The psychology of men's health

Christina Lee and R. Glynn Owens

Open University Press
Buckingham · Philadelphia

Open University Press
Celtic Court
22 Ballmoor
Buckingham
MK18 1XW

email: enquiries@openup.co.uk
world wide web: www.openup.co.uk

and

325 Chestnut Street
Philadelphia, PA 19106, USA

First published 2002

A catalogue record of this book is available from the British Library

ISBN   0 335 20705 7 (pb)   0 335 20706 5 (hb)

Library of Congress Cataloging-in-Publication Data
Lee, Christina.
    The psychology of men's health / Christina Lee and R. Glynn Owens.
        p. cm. – (Health psychology)
    Includes bibliographical references and index.
    ISBN 0-335-20706-5 – ISBN 0-335-20705-7 (pbk.)
    1. Men–Health and hygiene.   2. Clinical health psychology.
3. Men–Mental health.   I. Owens, R. Glynn.   II. Title.   III. Series.

RA564.83 L44 2002
613'.04234'019–dc21   2001045771

Typeset by Graphicraft Limited, Hong Kong
Printed in Great Britain by Biddles Limited, Guildford and King's Lynn

Contents

 # Series editors' foreword

This series of books in health psychology is designed to support postgraduate and post-qualification studies in psychology, nursing, medicine and health-care sciences. It is also intended to be accessible at advanced undergraduate level. The framework in which the books are set is psychosocial, in contrast to biomedical or physiological systems or organic disease approaches. Health psychology is growing rapidly as a field of study and as a profession. Concerned as it is with the application of psychological theories and models in the promotion and maintenance of health, and the individual and interpersonal aspects of adaptive behaviour in illness and disability, health psychology has a wide remit and a potentially important part to play in the future.

This book, written by Christina Lee and Glynn Owens, is addressed to students and researchers in various disciplines in health psychology and in health professions. It challenges the taken-for-granted assumption that men's health is unproblematic and that men's ways of being in the world are determined by individual choice. The close link between research methods and theory development in the history of psychology has tended to produce a particular way of seeing the world and the individuals within it, which has had a powerful impact on our understanding of people. For example, the discipline's close alliance with the scientific method, in particular the measurement of observable behaviour, means that it is difficult to conceive of some topics other than in ways in which they have been measured. Perhaps the best example of this is the notion of intelligence, which is exemplified by the IQ test. As readers will probably be aware, this way of measuring intelligence was largely developed in relation to boys and men, and has been severely criticized in the way it appears to discriminate against girls and women and those from other cultures and backgrounds. In fact, feminist psychology has been critical of the way that traditional psychology has tended to treat the attributes and experiences of

women as 'other'. Feminist and critical psychologists have challenged notions that attempt to explain aspects of behaviour as located solely within
individuals. They have highlighted the role of social and cultural factors in
behaviours such as smoking and sexual relationships.

The growth in the popularity and acceptance of a range of qualitative
methods, such as discourse analysis, grounded theory and interpretative
phenomenological analysis, has opened the gate to different explanations of
behaviour and different understandings of the individual within society. It
is from this stance that Lee and Owens offer their analysis of men's health.
They are critical of the neglect of men's health issues by mainstream psychology. They highlight areas where there is little research or where research
is based on unproblematic acceptance of biological givens such as in the
limited and secondary role of fathers in childcare, where many researchers
have made assumptions that childcare is primarily a female endeavour.
Lee and Owens reveal the damaging health impact of cultural norms that
define men in terms of their physicality and lack of emotional expression.
They have taken a broad approach to the subject, accessing research from
psychology, sociology and anthropology to develop and support their
arguments. We regard this as a ground-breaking book which is likely to
spark debate and challenge accepted ways of thinking about men and men's
health. We believe that it will form the foundation for courses in gender
studies which look beyond reproductive health and illness.

Sheila Payne and Sandra Horn

 Preface

A major feature of the discipline of psychology has been its expansion over the years into more and wider fields of application, with concomitant developments in its theoretical scope and its breadth of methodology. Prominent among psychology's new fields of research and application have been the application of psychological principles in the field of health and illness, and the recognition of the impact of social and political values on psychological functioning.

Health psychology is now a vigorous, thriving discipline in its own right, enhancing our understanding of many health problems, and making significant contributions to prevention and treatment. Paralleling the growth in health psychology has been an increasing recognition of the interaction of psychology with social, political and economic factors. Increasingly it is being recognized that a psychology that neglects consideration of the environmental and social context is at best an incomplete psychology, one which fails to address variables which clearly impact on individual choices and on well-being. Human behaviour does not occur within a social vacuum, and an effective health psychology, in common with other applied areas of the discipline, will need to pay close attention to these influences.

Feminist analyses have shown us how social factors such as gender make a major contribution to our understanding of individual choices, and how these may impact on health and well-being. Such analyses, however, have largely focused on the experiences of women, pointing out how a capitalist and patriarchal system disadvantages women. This book extends that argument to suggest that the gender order and other social constructions also limit the choices and behaviours of the majority of men, and that this impacts on their health and their ability to access health-care services.

This book argues that the prevalent social discourses which construct a myth of men as independent, self-reliant and physically competent lead to a limitation of men's choices in ways which influence their health.

Contemporary notions of the 'new man' as egalitarian and flexible have, paradoxically, placed even more pressure on men by implying that men's gender-relevant behaviour is a purely personal choice. Recognition of the characteristics of the male gender role, and myths about masculinity, permits us to draw links between social constructions of masculinity and behaviours which negatively affect men's health. At the individual level, these include men's relative reluctance to seek help for medical and psychological problems; high level of involvement in risky behaviours including drug use, criminal and violent behaviour; and voluntary exposure to physical danger in sports and recreation. At a social level, the stereotype that men are involved primarily in public activities and in work which supports a family financially, rather than in domestic life, further restricts men's choices and behaviours. Also apparent are the impacts of myths about male sexuality and physical appearance, including social pressure towards heterosexual promiscuity and sexual violence, homophobia and its effects on male sexual expression and demonstration of affection, body image, disordered eating and the abuse of steroids.

Modern society is characterized by long-term unemployment, casualization of the workforce, decreased leisure time, high rates of family breakup, and highly variable family structures; yet the social myth of the nuclear family, and the concept that a man should support a wife and children financially through a full-time permanent career outside the home, continues to influence expectations no matter how untenable in practice. This discrepancy between expectation and reality forms a potent source of stress with significant health implications including particular issues which confront ageing men.

The aim of this book, therefore, is to argue for a gendered approach to research on men, and to suggest directions for the development of a psychology of men's health. Only by doing so, it is argued, will psychology achieve a meaningful and effective view of the experience of men in society today, and identify targets for change that would serve to maximize the well-being of both men and women.

CHAPTER I

Gender and men's health

Research in both psychology and health has traditionally focused on men to the neglect of women. So why do we need a book on the psychology of men's health? It is unquestionably the case that psychological research and theory have overwhelmingly focused on men's lives and men's experiences, and that psychology – in common with other scientific fields – has assumed that men's experiences and perspectives are normative in a way that women's are not.

But the effects of the gendered nature of society on men's health and well-being have largely been ignored by mainstream psychologists. Although men may have been the centre of attention, implicitly or explicitly regarded as the 'norm' from which women are to a greater or lesser extent deviant or inferior, men have not been studied from the perspective of gender: what, other than biology, does it mean to be a man in contemporary society, and how might social and cultural expectations of masculinity affect men's behaviour, their expectations, their relationships, and their physical and emotional health?

Disciplines such as sociology, history and cultural studies have long ago developed an awareness of the gendered nature of men's experience, of the artificial nature of social definitions of 'masculine' behaviours and attitudes, and of the effects that gender stereotypes have on men's well-being (for example Pleck 1976; Brod 1987; Segal 1990; Brod and Kaufman 1994; Connell 1995; Mac an Ghaill 1996; Petersen 1998). But these developments have not been reflected in the discipline of psychology, which continues to lack any coherent body of research on gender issues as they impinge on the lives of men.

Psychological research can be criticized for assuming an artificially gender-neutral perspective on human behaviour. Mainstream psychology either treats systemic gender inequities in income, social responsibilities, social power, and access to resources as natural and inevitable, or assumes them to be irrelevant to understanding individual behaviour. Criticisms such as these have frequently been made in commentaries on the psychology of women's health (for example Landrine 1995; Burman *et al.* 1996; Lee 1998a). Equally, however, a psychology of men's health can usefully address the social construction of masculinities and the effects that gender roles, stereotypes and myths about appropriate behaviour for men have on men's lifestyles and behaviours, and thus their health.

The aim of this book, then, is to explore aspects of the gendered nature of society as they impinge on the behaviour and well-being of individual men. The psychology of men's health is a field in its infancy. Even researchers who are primarily interested in social concepts of gender and their effects on health have tended to focus on women, and to neglect the questions of how men come to behave as they do (Watson 2000). Thus, much of the argument and evidence presented in this book is an extension of feminist work on the psychology of women's health, or derived from other disciplines such as sociology and demography. The book aims to set an agenda, to raise awareness of important issues for men's well-being and to suggest a direction for the development of the psychology of men's health which has as its fundamental aim the liberation of both men and women from restrictive and unnecessary gender roles. This is an explicitly political aim, but we argue later in this chapter that all psychological research is political: that which does not seek to produce social change is politically conservative, not neutral.

Patriarchy and masculinity

Human cultures, almost universally, construct men's interests and concerns as more legitimate and more central than women's (Millett 1970). This perspective might be seen as unambiguously advantageous to men, but this book aims to question this assumption, and to demonstrate that patriarchy is not necessarily advantageous to all, or indeed to any, men.

It is certainly the case that patriarchy disadvantages women, and it is easy to assume that what is bad for women must be good for men, but this is by no means the only conclusion that can be reached. Debates about gender in general have often been predicated on this assumption: social changes that benefit women must be to the detriment of men. A zero-sum model is assumed, in which one gender can benefit only at the expense of the other. We reject this point of view, arguing throughout this book that a sympathetic and gendered understanding of the lives of men does not have negative implications for women. On the contrary, recognition of the limitations of gender-based roles and stereotypes, and exploration of alternative social arrangements, has the potential to produce healthy outcomes for both men and women.

Later chapters in this book explore the influence of socially constructed gender roles on men's health. We argue that men are, to a greater or lesser degree, caught between the demands of two sets of expectations, neither of which is readily compatible with contemporary social realities (Copenhaver and Eisler 1996). Theorists of masculinity generally argue that it is necessary to recognize multiple 'masculinities' in order to understand the lives of men from a range of ethnic backgrounds, social classes and sexual orientations (for example Connell 1995; Mac an Ghaill 1996). This book, however, concentrates on two main social constructions of how men should behave. We contrast the traditionally dominant model of masculinity which Connell (1998) refers to as 'hegemonic masculinity' – that model of masculinity which society privileges as 'true' maleness – with modern, egalitarian perspectives on men's 'new' gender roles. Our argument is that neither of these is unproblematic for men, or for the women and children with whom they share their lives.

'Hegemonic masculinity' refers to the traditional, patriarchal view of men and men's behaviour, which is arguably the most influential and the most restrictive of masculinities, defining as it does culturally accepted notions of 'real' manhood. This social construction is highly prescriptive. It defines a 'real' man as essentially – that is, in essence, fundamentally, inevitably and unchangeably – different from a woman. A man is characterized by toughness, unemotionality, physical competence, competitiveness and aggression. According to this model, men must compete to demonstrate their superiority to other men: to be successful is to have possessions and characteristics that make one envied by other men.

By contrast, modern views of gender relations and the 'new' man downplay differences between the sexes, recognizing that many traditionally gendered aspects of life are purely arbitrary, and prescribing that men should find more egalitarian ways of interacting with women. While this perspective appears more equitable, in that it assumes that men and women are equally able to contribute to society in a range of different ways and that a person may be happy and successful without adhering strictly to a rigid gender role, it generally fails to take into account the material and systemic realities which restrict the choices of both men and women. It focuses on the individual and neglects economic, cultural and social forces, ignoring the fact that individual choices about behaviour and lifestyle are rarely entirely free of constraint, and are always influenced by gender expectations.

Traditional, hegemonic definitions of masculinity prescribe certain behaviours as appropriate for men, and others as completely inappropriate. Powerful social sanctions come into play against individuals who transgress social expectations for these gender-appropriate behaviours, and these are sufficiently strong to counteract both the obvious gender inequities inherent in traditional behaviour patterns and the recognized health risks associated with many of these behaviours. This book explores some of these behaviours, both at the level of the individual man and at the level of his relations with families and broader society, and it also explores the problems faced by men who want to alter their patterns of behaviour. At the individual level, these behaviours include men's relative reluctance to seek help for medical and psychological problems; avoidance of the expression of emotion; aggressive and unsafe sexual behaviours and attitudes; and high level of involvement in risky behaviours, which include both the socially sanctioned risks involved in physically dangerous sports and recreational activities and the more deviant masculine-typed risks such as crime and violent behaviour. At a social level, unhealthy gender-related behaviours arise from pressures on men to identify themselves and their value in terms of their paid work roles, and to avoid involvement in family activities. We argue that these patterns of behaviour can all be seen as arising from hegemonic masculinity and the internalization of the values associated with it.

Dominant social discourses position men's life choices – concerning work, family and recreation – as freely chosen individual behaviours, and implicitly blame individual men who make risky or antisocial choices, or who suffer physically or emotionally as a result of these choices. The existence of an alternative, egalitarian, model of men's behaviour is taken as evidence that individual men have made a free choice to adopt traditional masculine roles, and that any resulting illness or injury is thus the individual's responsibility. There is little awareness among psychologists, or in society more generally, of the role of social constructions surrounding concepts of gender in restricting men's choices, nor is there much awareness of the gendered nature of social institutions such as educational, employment and legal systems which make it difficult for men and women to choose other-gender-typed behaviours. Although the 'new' man is a familiar social role, we argue that adopting this egalitarian role exposes men to social stigma and to a sense of inferiority which is psychologically uncomfortable; thus, egalitarian attitudes and behaviours become prohibitively difficult to sustain.

Social construction of masculinity and the psychology of men's health

The central issue for this book, then, is the social construction of gender as it impinges on the behaviour of men and thus on their physical and emotional health. From a psychological point of view, the unique aspects of men's health are those which are affected by men's social roles, and not purely by their biology. This book explores the ways in which social myths and stereotypes about appropriate or 'natural' behaviour for men impact on their well-being.

An emphasis on social contexts and their impact on men's lives also means that a focus on specific illnesses and risk factors is less important than an analysis which deals primarily with the essentially social nature of gender and of sex roles. There is a widespread assumption that research on men's health should focus primarily on diseases which occur among men. The authors' conversations with academics, policy-makers and service providers on the topic of men's health usually produce the response, 'ah yes, prostate cancer'. While it is true that prostate cancer is an important cause of death among men, it is arguable that from a psychological point of view, men's experiences of prostate cancer are not particularly different from the experiences of men or women with cancer more generally. While there is obviously a sex difference in the prevalence of types of cancer (American Cancer Society 1994), it is by no means clear that there is a specific and essential gender difference in people's psychological reactions to cancer diagnosis and treatment. Thus, from a psychological point of view, what is important is not that men get prostate cancer and women get breast cancer: it is that men's and women's lives, the contexts within which they experience cancer, are very different from each other.

More generally, a focus on disease is an overly biological perspective for a psychology that focuses on the man as a person. More important for men's health than any individual disease is the influence of social constructions of maleness. It is the extent to which these social constructions tend to lead to men choosing behaviours which shorten their life expectancy or reduce their quality of life that is the focus of this book. In order to understand the psychology of men and of men's health, men have to be understood in a complex social and cultural context. As Watson (2000) has argued, it is masculinity, rather than maleness, which shortens men's lives and reduces their well-being.

The book examines issues that are relevant to the everyday lives of all men throughout their lifespans, rather than focusing on illness, death and specific 'health behaviours' as so much health psychology has done. While the experiences of men undergoing treatment for cancer, substance abuse or HIV/AIDS are important topics, the emphasis here is on everyday life rather than on major health crises. The book explores men's experiences as workers, fathers, and as members of society, demonstrating the ways in which social assumptions about masculinity influence every aspect of men's lives, their physical and emotional health, and their life expectancy.

Outline of the book

The first part of this book explores men's individual health-related behaviours in an effort to understand why men's life expectancies are lower than women's in almost all cultures. Chapter 2 explores men's lower use of health care and screening services, and their relative reluctance to adopt health-related behaviours. Chapter 3 extends this argument to examine men's reluctance to seek help for emotional problems, placing this in the context of well-established cultural barriers to men's expression of emotions (Brody 1999), and thus to men's opportunities to articulate emotional distress appropriately. Chapter 4 examines risk-taking and exposure to violence as an important but under-studied contributor to men's lower life expectancy, again considering the role of gendered expectations of behaviour in influencing men's tendency to choose to behave in ways that put them at risk of injury or death. Chapter 5 extends this perspective further, examining the role of social expectations on men's sexual behaviour and the effects that these have on men's physical and emotional well-being. Chapter 6 explores men's relationships with their bodies more generally, exploring men's body image and the effects of injunctions on men to be large, strong and physically competent, despite the fact that few men in contemporary society have any practical need to meet this cultural expectation.

The second part of the book shifts the focus from individual behaviours to social roles and to men in context. The social roles prescribed by hegemonic masculinity are as constrained as are the individual behaviours, and are also demonstrably associated with low levels of physical and emotional health. In particular, hegemonic models of masculinity provide prescriptive and limiting perspectives on men's family roles. Men are positioned almost exclusively as material providers whose personal characteristics and relationships with their partners and children are peripheral and unimportant.

In societies which are increasingly characterized by long-term unemployment, casualization of the workforce, decreased leisure time, high rates of family breakup, and highly variable family structures (for example US Bureau of Labor Statistics 1991), this expectation is increasingly untenable. Yet it continues to influence both men's and women's concepts of successful masculinity (Coltrane 1989). Men continue to be defined in terms of the status of their paid employment and their success in providing financially for their families. This discrepancy between expectation and reality forms a potent source of stress with significant implications for physical and emotional well-being (for example Smith 1998).

Chapter 7, therefore, focuses on the relationships between men and the workforce. Chapter 8 explores men's relationships with their families, stressing the extent to which men's emotional relationships and family roles have been excluded from psychological research, to the detriment of those men and of a full understanding of contemporary family life. In Chapter 9, we explore the gendered meanings of ageing for men, and the final chapter points to some directions for the development of psychology of men's health. We argue that this development is best served by an understanding of masculinity that is explicitly political, and that takes social contexts and gendered expectations into account. Further, we argue that psychology has been singularly unsuccessful to date in providing useful models of individual choices in the context of gendered social forces, and that the broadening of psychology to encompass social realities requires the broadening of research methods as well.

Research methods in the psychology of men's health

Despite psychology's aspirations to the value-neutral methods and models of classical physics, this book is based on the assumption that individual men's behavioural choices cannot be understood without an appreciation of their sociocultural contexts (Fox and Prilleltensky 1997). Traditionally, psychology has attempted to remove individual behaviour from its social context and study it in isolation in the laboratory. This epistemological perspective regards context as a 'contaminant' to be controlled, rather than as an essential aspect of the behaviour. Some theorists, however, argue that such an approach misses the point for a great deal of social behaviour, and that contextualism – an epistemology which emphasizes the importance of studying behaviour in its context (for example Jaeger and Rosnow 1988; Biglan *et al.* 1990) – is more appropriate for most social behaviour. This would appear to be particularly the case in understanding gendered behaviour, which can be understood only in the context of a gendered society.

It is also important to stress that research involving human beings is inevitably political (Prilleltensky 1989). Research into men's health that ignores the social context, or that treats it as a neutral background or as an inevitable aspect of an immutable reality, is politically conservative, seeking solutions to men's problems in individual adaptation rather than in social change (Bailey and Eastman 1994; Kipnis 1994). Conversely, a psychology of men's health that starts from the perspective that masculinity is socially constructed and mutable is inevitably oriented towards social explanations and social solutions to the problems of individual lives – approaches which reflect both Marx's 'The philosophers have only interpreted the world in various ways: the point, however, is to change it' (1963: 84) and Skinner's '. . . the problems we face are not to be found in men and women, but in the world in which they live' (1975: 49).

Wilkinson (1996) has argued that a psychology of women's health is strengthened by the application of a variety of epistemologies, in order to develop a fully rounded understanding of individual behaviour at all levels of explanation. The same may be argued for a psychology of men's health. There is certainly a role in the psychology of men's health for traditional empiricist science, and the psychology of men's health can certainly benefit by adopting the principles of 'feminist empiricism'. This approach makes use of traditional scientific methods, with their emphasis on objectivity, replicability and experimental control, but aims to develop hypotheses, and interpret findings, with a conscious avoidance of sexist assumptions about how men or women should behave, think or feel. Writers focusing on the psychology of women from this perspective (for example McHugh *et al.* 1986; Denmark *et al.* 1988) have discussed strategies for avoiding sexism through attention to women's perspectives, including the inclusion of female research participants and of topics of particular relevance to women, avoidance of inappropriate over-generalization from male research samples, and avoidance of the interpretation of gender differences as evidence of the inferiority of women.

In researching the psychology of men's health, a feminist empiricist approach would involve an acknowledgement that hegemonic models of masculinity do not necessarily describe the experiences of the majority of men, nor do they represent appropriate ideals for all or indeed any men. It would seek to explore the experiences of men in non-traditional areas such as parenthood and family relationships, and those of men who lead personal or occupational lives that do not conform to traditional notions of 'appropriate' masculine behaviour.

For example, research based on assumptions that all men are, or should aspire to be, physically strong, emotionally independent, aggressive, heterosexual, gainfully employed, providers for nuclear families who avoid all activities associated with children or the home, reinforces stereotyped notions about men (Petersen 1998). Research which treats men's desire to care for their own children as abnormal, or pathologizes men who choose to work in nursing or childcare, or assumes that men without paid employment must necessarily lack meaningful social roles, reinforces traditional and restrictive attitudes towards men and their choices.

Conversely, feminist empiricist research in the psychology of men's health might usefully problematize negative and traditionally masculine characteristics such as excessive self-esteem, or homophobia, or inexpressiveness, characteristics that contribute to poor interpersonal relationships but which traditional models of masculinity position as positive and desirable for men. Research which explores strategies for improving men's emotional expression and nurturing behaviour, or which seeks to discourage sexual coercion or unnecessary physical risk-taking among young men, also undermines gender-based stereotypes and provides alternative models of successful masculinity (Caplan and Caplan 1999).

Feminist empiricist research methods are likely to be acceptable to mainstream psychology, because they share the values of objectivity and experimental control which are central to empiricist psychology. However, the psychology of men's health is also likely to benefit from the use of qualitative, constructivist and contextualist methodologies (for example Watson 2000). These strategies are based on epistemologies which do not attempt to achieve experimental control or to remove the event under investigation from its context. Rather, they take the individual-in-context as the basic unit of analysis and examine the role of social structures, social expectations, and social constructions in the development of individual patterns of behaviour (Striegel-Moore 1994).

Qualitative and exploratory methods, such as focus groups, semi-structured interviews and participant observation, enable men's health to be explored from the perspective of men who are living a gendered life. Watson (2000), for example, used a series of interviews with Scottish men over several years to explore their health, their relationships with their bodies and their experience of ageing in order to develop a richly informative description of men's lives from the inside. Methods such as these have the potential to develop an inclusive and socially relevant psychology of men's health, by enabling researchers to explore 'difficult' issues. Research, for example, on partner abuse in gay relationships, on men in role-reversed households, or on men's adjustment to divorce, involves men who are in stigmatized situations. Traditional quantitative methods may not be successful in attracting research volunteers or encouraging them to describe their experiences. A participatory research model, in which the participants are approached as equal partners in the research process, with a voice in the design of the investigation and the use to which the findings are put, may be the only way in which it is possible to establish the extent to which such phenomena produce serious problems for men's physical or emotional health.

For this book, research from traditional empiricist and from alternative epistemologies is presented together in order to build a comprehensive perspective on men's behaviours and attitudes. The psychology of men's health is in its infancy, and at this stage it is most useful to be as inclusive as possible, exploring a variety of perspectives on each issue. While these perspectives may be so different from each other as to be at times completely incommensurable, the consideration of all of them is essential in beginning the process of developing a fully articulated psychology of men's health.

Summary

◆ While psychological and health research has traditionally focused on men to the exclusion of women, the work has not generally been informed by a gender perspective. The psychology of men's health aims to provide this analysis.
◆ Men's health, and men's choices about health-related behaviours, must be understood in the context of patriarchal societal structures. Patriarchy, with its assumptions that men and men's concerns are more central and important than are women, may be seen as unproblematically advantageous to men, but is in fact almost as restrictive for men as for women.
◆ Implicit in patriarchy is a traditional model of masculinity which prescribes that men are must conform to a particular stereotype: to be strong, unemotional, aggressive, competitive and unconcerned with family life. This 'hegemonic' model of masculinity supports individual behaviours which compromise men's health.
◆ Sociologists of masculinity identify a range of masculinities, encompassing the experiences of men from different ethnic backgrounds, social classes and sexual orientations. This book contrasts traditional, hegemonic, conceptions of masculinity with contemporary and egalitarian models

of the 'new' man. It argues that the existence of complementary models of masculinity gives the illusion that individual men have a choice in their behaviours, but that the egalitarian modes of behaviour are negatively valued and that individual choices are not unconstrained by social pressures.

♦ Sociocultural expectations of masculine behaviour influence men to choose behaviours and lifestyles which are unhealthy for them and for their families, yet the influence of sociocultural concepts of masculinity have largely been ignored and individual men have been blamed for making unhealthy choices.

♦ Men's health must be understood in the context of men's lives. This book focuses on aspects of everyday life, such as work and family, rather than on individual diseases.

♦ In understanding men's health in the context of their lives, it is necessary to broaden the range of epistemologies adopted by psychology. While traditional empiricism has undoubted strengths, alternative qualitative approaches allow one to see individual behaviours in a broader context and to develop a fuller understanding of the constraints on individual choice.

Additional reading

Connell, R.W. (1995) *Masculinities*. Sydney: Allen & Unwin.
Petersen, A. (1998) *Unmasking the Masculine: 'Men' and 'Identity' in a Sceptical Age*. London: Sage.
Watson, J. (2000) *Male Bodies: Health, Culture and Identity*. Buckingham: Open University Press.

Health behaviours and health service use

One of the most well-established gender differences in health is that men's life expectancy, worldwide, averages 3 years less than women's (Population Reference Bureau 2000). It is perhaps less widely recognized that the size of the gender gap varies greatly between regions. In Eastern Europe, for example, men's life expectancy is 11 years less than women's, while by contrast, men's life expectancy is equal to or greater than women's in countries such as Afghanistan, in which religious, cultural and legal institutions ensure that women do not have adequate access to health and social services. In developed countries, men can generally expect about 8 years of life less than women (Population Reference Bureau 2000).

There is considerable debate about the causes of the difference in life expectancy. While it is widely assumed that men are biologically predisposed to earlier death, the range of differentials between regions and populations make it clear that cultural, social, environmental and behavioural factors must play a major role. In Australia, for example, the life expectancy of indigenous men is 19 years less than that of non-indigenous men and 23 years less than that of non-indigenous women (Anderson *et al.* 1996), a difference which seems far too large to be explained entirely by biological differences in susceptibility to disease.

Males are certainly biologically less robust than females, as is demonstrated by consistently higher neonatal death rates among males than females. In Australia, for example, the neonatal death rate is 3.4 per thousand live births for males, compared with only 2.5 per thousand for females (Australian Bureau of Statistics 1996a). These differences so early in life must find their explanation in biological differences, but the role of sociocultural factors is demonstrable for other causes of death. To take a well-researched example of gender differences, coronary heart disease is second to cancer as the leading cause of death for both men and women in most developed countries (for example Australian Bureau of Statistics 2000), but men die of

coronary heart disease younger than women. Explanations for this difference may be found in biological, behavioural and sociocultural factors. At a
biological level, men lack the protective effect of oestrogen which improves
lipid profiles and reduces risk of cardiovascular disease in pre-menopausal
women (Dubbert and Martin 1988). At the same time, cultural institutions
and assumptions about masculinity encourage men to internalize attitudes
and adopt behaviours that increase risk of coronary heart disease. At an
attitudinal level these include hostile and competitive views of social relationships, while at a behavioural level they include high-fat, high-alcohol
diets. These attitudes and behaviours are consistent with hegemonic views
of masculinity and are chosen by men at least in part because they enable
them to enact a socially constructed 'male script', but at the same time they
are associated with increased cardiovascular mortality (Helgeson 1995).

   Popular culture generally fails to recognize the influence of cultural and
social factors on health behaviour and on life expectancy. When behavioural
and attitudinal differences are acknowledged, they are often treated in an
essentialist manner, with the assumption that men are 'naturally' predisposed
to behave in ways which cause them to wear out earlier. These predisposi-
tions are frequently put down to the inescapable effects of testosterone,
despite evidence that the effects of testosterone on behaviour are variable
and situation dependent (Archer et al. 1998); thus it is assumed that there is
no need to attempt to explain or reduce this difference.

   A survey of US adults showed that men and women tended to attribute
differences in longevity differently: men tend to believe that differences in
life expectancy arise because men work harder and experience more stress,
while women are more likely to believe that it is because men do not take
as good care of their health (Wallace 1996). The empirical evidence tends to
support the female view on this matter. The popular belief that men have
higher workloads than women is consistent with a cultural stereotype of
masculinity which positions men primarily as workers and as essentially
tougher and more hard-working than women (Petersen 1998). Nevertheless, there is consistent evidence that women, not men, have higher workloads and longer working hours (Bittman and Lovejoy 1993). Women also
have higher levels of self-reported stress (Davis et al. 1999). Thus, men's
shorter life expectancy cannot be attributed to overwork or stress in a
straightforward manner.

   There is, however, evidence that other aspects of hegemonic masculinity
do affect men's health attitudes and behaviours, pressuring them to choose
to act in ways which are harmful to their health and which tend to reduce
life expectancy. The evidence that men lead less healthy lifestyles than
women (reviewed briefly below) is well established. It has not, however,
generally been interpreted from a perspective that acknowledges the social
pressures on men to conform to unhealthy gender-based stereotypes. While
there are some exceptions, such as the work of Watson (2000), who
explored men's experiences of their bodies from a qualitative perspective,

there is a general view that men are not disadvantaged by their gender roles. Thus, men's low levels of health-protective behaviours (discussed below) and high levels of risk-taking (discussed in Chapter 4) are interpreted at an individual level. Men who make less than optimal health choices are positioned, not as victims of cultural pressures, but as individuals who have freely chosen to behave in self-destructive ways. This lack of acknowledgement of the constraints on men's choices with reference to health behaviour leads to a blaming of the victims of cultural and social influences. It has meant a historical lack of efforts to improve men's health behaviours, an assumption that such efforts will inevitably be unsuccessful, and a general perspective that men who behave in ways which compromise their health have made a free and unconstrained choice to do so (Courtenay 1998). Thus, men are seen as personally at fault if their health behaviour is less than optimal. This view may be contrasted with social perspectives on women's health, which readily acknowledge the influence of social pressure. Women's unhealthy dietary patterns, for example, are widely acknowledged as influenced by cultural stereotypes, and women are positioned as the victims of social expectations (for example Ussher 1997); parallel explanations of men's health-related choices are almost nonexistent.

Gender and health behaviours

Hegemonic models of gender position a concern for one's health as a feminine characteristic; men are positioned as 'naturally' strong, resistant to disease, unresponsive to pain and physical distress, and unconcerned with minor symptoms (Petersen 1998). Courtenay (2000) and Waldron (1997) are among the few scholars of gender and health to have argued that gender-related differences in health beliefs and behaviours contribute significantly to the differences in life expectancy. Sociocultural forces encourage men to engage in stereotypically masculine behaviour in order to differentiate themselves as much as possible from women, and the resources which men and boys use to enact gender are largely unhealthy. Thus, the causes of gender differences in health behaviour arise from men's being socialized to disregard knowledge about healthy lifestyles and to choose harmful behaviours, as one way of acting out the male script, while women are socialized to be cautious with their own health and protective of the health of others.

Consistent with these arguments, population surveys from a range of countries and age groups demonstrate overwhelmingly that men engage in more health-damaging behaviours and women in more health-protective behaviours (for example Uitenbroek *et al.* 1996; Stronegger *et al.* 1997). In particular, men are less likely than women to moderate their dietary fat (Katz *et al.* 1998) and alcohol intake (Holtzman *et al.* 2000) and to maintain a healthy body weight (Holtzman *et al.* 2000). Surveys from Europe and the USA demonstrate consistently that gender differences in health behaviour are particularly strong in areas to do with eating and food choice (for example Reime *et al.* 2000), an aspect of life which is strongly female-typed in almost all cultures. The only health-promoting behaviour which is consistently engaged in by men more than by women is physical activity (Dubbert and Martin 1988), an activity which is consistent with the identification of hegemonic masculinity with the tough, disciplined and athletic body (Petersen 1998).

Men are also less likely than women to express an interest in making health-related lifestyle changes (Gabhainn *et al.* 1999); young men are likely to see little point in changing risk behaviours 'yet', while older men express the view that at their age it is 'too late' for behavioural changes to have any effect on health. Unfortunately, neither of these attitudes is consistent with the empirical evidence: health behaviours in younger and middle adulthood are strong predictors of longevity and of well-being in older age, while healthy lifestyles among older men also predict longevity and are associated with improved quality of life (Davis *et al.* 1994). But these self-harming attitudes are consistent with a 'male script' that places value on a disregard for the long-term health consequences of one's actions and that views taking care of one's body as evidence that one is 'soft' or of a feminine (possibly homosexual) concern for appearance (Petersen 1998).

Courtenay (1998) has argued that the health of young men in particular deserves more attention than it receives. As Chapter 4 demonstrates, young men are disproportionately at risk of injury and accidental death (Smith 1993); they have low levels of health-promoting behaviour and high rates of risky behaviours, which are encouraged by socially mediated beliefs about 'masculine' behaviour and by an illogical but pervasive sense of personal invulnerability. For example, Lonnquist *et al.* (1992) found that male college students averaged fewer health-promoting behaviours than females, and that males' rates of healthy behaviour tended to decrease during their college years while females' tended to increase. Consistent with research with other populations and with stereotypical notions of male and female concerns, Welsh *et al.* (1998) found that the attitudes and behaviours of male college students which did relate to the maintenance of health tended to focus on physical activity, while female students' health concerns focused on diet. Courtenay (1998) has argued that young men should not be dismissed as wilfully negligent of their health, but that the effects of sociocultural influences must be recognized. Thus, gender-specific health interventions are needed to help young men make the transition to adulthood safely.

Men know less about health and healthy lifestyles than women, and cultural institutions position women, rather than men themselves, as responsible for men's health. Lyons and Willott (1999), for example, have analysed the way in which the popular media direct information about men's health and health behaviours towards their wives and mothers, establishing and reinforcing the notion that men should not concern themselves with health issues and indeed are incapable of caring for their own health. Consistent with this cultural expectation, Umberson (1992) demonstrated that, following marriage, women tended to make efforts to control health-related aspects of their husbands' behaviour, but men did not attempt to control those aspects of their wives' behaviour. Loss of a partner, whether through divorce (Umberson 1992) or widowhood (Clayton 1990), is associated with more negative changes in health behaviours for men than it is for women, particular those behaviours associated with diet and with use of alcohol and other drugs (Byrne *et al.* 1999).

Women's culturally determined willingness to take care of men's health may appear, like other aspects of a patriarchal society, to benefit men, but in fact the cultural prescription that men should be ignorant of health-promoting behaviour and unable to look after their own health serves to undermine men's independence and reduce their freedom to make lifestyle choices. It also means that men who do not have a female partner may experience avoidable ill health and shortened life expectancy, and that men who do concern themselves with their health may be stigmatized.

Gender, health service use and subjective health

Compounding the problem that men's lifestyles tend to be less healthy than women's is evidence that men make less use of health care and screening services than women (for example Schappert 1999) and are slower to acknowledge symptoms of illness (for example Gijsbers van Wijk *et al.* 1999). This effect is found even when the effects of gynaecological services are accounted for (for example Stoverinck *et al.* 1996). The aspect of health service use which most clearly and unequivocally demonstrates the expected gender imbalance is in the use of psychological services. The requirement that men should be independent, strong, self-reliant and emotionally restrained makes it particularly difficult for men to seek psychological services (Levant 1996). While boys are more likely than girls to be taken to a psychologist by parents or referred by teachers, men are less likely than women to seek psychological services for themselves (Jorm 1994). The impact that this relative reluctance to discuss emotional issues may have on men's well-being is discussed in detail in Chapter 3.

The arguments presented so far in this chapter would lead to the assumption that the majority of men are influenced by cultural stereotypes to ignore physical symptoms, to be unconcerned about screening and preventive health care, and to delay help-seeking for symptoms. There is a tendency to attribute men's behaviour in this respect to biological factors. Men, for example, are popularly supposed to have a higher pain threshold than women. The evidence on this, however, indicates that sex and gender differences in pain thresholds are complex and depend on measurement techniques, situations and expectancies as much as they do on physiological factors (Miaskowski 1999). The inadequacy of biological explanations for men's lower use of health services is demonstrated by research showing that variation in health-care use and symptom recognition is largely explained by the effects of socio-economic and work-related variables.

Emslie *et al.* (1999a), for example, found small but consistent gender differences in malaise and physical symptoms between male and female university employees, but found that the effects of occupational grade and working conditions were far more important in predicting these variables. Thus, gender differences in subjective health are explained not by biological maleness, but by the behaviours and attitudes which are associated with particular careers and lifestyle choices. Very much the same effect was found in a similar survey of bank employees (Emslie *et al.* 1999b); in this survey, women reported higher levels of malaise, though there were no differences in physical symptoms, but working conditions and occupational grade were again far more important predictors than the sex of the respondent. While large-scale research with British public servants showed that women were more likely than men to take time off work for illness, these effects were small and again strongly influenced by occupational grade (Feeney *et al.* 1998). Taken together, these surveys suggest that gender differences in subjective well-being and symptom reporting do not arise from essential biological differences between men and women, but from social and employment conditions which may affect people's relationships with their bodies and their health.

There is other evidence, however, which does not fit well with the arguments developed in this chapter so far. A survey of the general population in Scotland (Macintyre *et al.* 1999) found no evidence for the hypothesis that men were in general less willing than women to report symptoms or to seek health care, or that men were reluctant to report symptoms that were 'trivial' or emotional in nature. Another survey by the same group (Wyke *et al.* 1998) found that men were less likely than women to report a range of symptoms, but that those who did report symptoms were just as likely to have seen a doctor about them. A study of men and women with colds (Macintyre 1993) even found that men were actually more likely to overrate the severity of their symptoms, by comparison with an objective clinical observer, than were women.

The conflicting nature of these findings requires some explanation. There is good evidence that men generally have less healthy lifestyles than women and make less use of health services. By contrast, gender differences in self-rated health are small and can generally be explained by occupational and social factors. One important point to be made is that hegemonic masculinity (Connell 1995) or the 'male code' (Levant 1996) is prescriptive rather than descriptive. That is, it specifies what a man should be in order to embody the stereotype of the successful male in a patriarchal society, rather than describing what real men do in real circumstances. The private nature of symptoms and subjective health experiences may be contrasted with the publicly visible nature of health behaviours and health service use, and this may offer an explanation. Men may adopt behaviours that are consistent with cultural expectations without necessarily internalizing all aspects of the male code; thus their public health behaviours and their private health experiences may conflict.

Kandrack *et al.* (1991) have argued that research which simply compares men and women on counts of health service use is of limited use, and that in order to understand gender differences in use of health service, there should be a shift in focus from who goes to the doctor to the reasons they have for going, what actually happens during the consultation, and what treatment is provided or recommended. From the perspective of improving men's health behaviours and encouraging them to take personal responsibility for the care of their bodies, a research agenda which focuses on the circumstances under which men do seek help and the types of interventions and consultation styles which are effective with men could play a major role in improving men's well-being and perhaps life expectancy.

Conclusion

Men are less likely than women to engage in almost all health-promoting behaviours, with the notable exception of physical activity; while the evidence is less clear on this point, they generally make less use of health services and may be less willing to report symptoms or have screening checks. Cultural assumptions about masculinity and femininity include the stereotypes that men should be strong, stoical and insensitive to pain, and that women should take responsibility for the health and health behaviours of the men in their lives. These stereotypes disempower men and reduce their ability to lead long, healthy lives.

This chapter demonstrates that a significant proportion of the difference in longevity between men and women is explicable in terms of culturally mediated attitudes and individual behaviours. Yet mainstream psychology is silent on this issue, or simply makes the assumption that men are intrinsically uninterested in their own health and longevity and that there is no point in trying to intervene to change men's attitudes or behaviours. Health psychology lacks a critical approach to gender differences in general, and in particular to the factors which influence health-damaging choices among men. Men's health and health behaviour have yet to be identified as a gender issue. Yet it is one which must be addressed. Gender differences in life expectancy are perhaps the most dramatic example of the need for a stronger focus on men's health, and for a greater understanding of the social and cultural pressures which encourage men to choose lifestyles which reduce both the quality and the quantity of their lives.

Summary

♦ Men's life expectancies are shorter than women's in almost all countries, but the size of the gender gap varies greatly and is affected by social and political systems.
♦ Gender differences in life expectancy may be explained by attitudinal and behavioural differences, rather than biological factors.
♦ Men make less use than women of health services and are also less likely to engage in health-promoting behaviours.
♦ Concern for one's health and interest in health matters, especially those concerned with diet, are positioned as intrinsically feminine in most cultures. Information about men's health is frequently directed to women, who are expected to take responsibility for men's health as well as their own.
♦ Men's unhealthy behaviours are popularly ascribed to individual choice, and there is little acknowledgement of social and cultural influences that identify successful masculinity with a lack of concern for one's health.
♦ Interventions to improve men's health behaviours and health service use need to address cultural stereotypes and acknowledge the constraints on individual men's choices in order to improve their well-being and life expectancy.

Additional reading

Courtenay, W.H. (2000) Engendering health: a social constructionist examination of men's health beliefs and behaviors, *Psychology of Men and Masculinity*, 1: 4–15.
Watson, J. (2000) *Male Bodies: Health, Culture and Identity*. Buckingham: Open University Press.

CHAPTER 3

Emotional expression

One of the central tenets of hegemonic masculinity is that a man should be strong, silent and self-contained: a man should not express his emotions openly, and should not share his emotions with other people or ask for help when experiencing emotional distress (Petersen 1998). This is one aspect of prescriptive definitions of masculinity that has been extensively explored from a range of perspective by psychologists and social theorists. For example, Lupton (1998) has explored the gendered nature of emotionality from a historical and sociocultural viewpoint, while Brody (1999) has explored much the same territory from a perspective which draws extensively on evidence from mainstream experimental psychology. Despite fundamental differences in epistemologies, both authors reach very similar conclusions. They draw on evidence to demonstrate that men express emotions, particularly negative internally focused emotions (for example grief) and positive externally focused emotions (for example tenderness) to a considerably lesser degree than do women. The evidence indicates strongly that this difference is culturally rather than biologically determined, and also shows that this relative lack of emotional expression is, in general, detrimental to physical and emotional well-being. Both writers, also, demonstrate that cultural stereotypes of gender differences in emotional expression do not always reflect reality, tending to exaggerate the extent of actual gender differences.

Lupton (1998) is one of several commentators to have described the social stereotype of the unemotional man, in contrast with the emotional woman, in some detail. Patriarchal cultures, she argues, position mastery over the emotions as a positive and valuable thing for men. Men who express their emotions openly are stigmatized as weak, effeminate and (possibly) homosexual. By contrast, women are expected to show less control over their emotions: for women, failure to express emotions is construed as evidence of unwomanliness and a 'hard', unsympathetic nature.

Lupton's (1998) deconstruction of this asymmetry has focused mainly on the point of view of women. She has argued that women's assumed 'natural' emotionality is a concept which carries complex cultural baggage: on one level, emotionality is construed as a positive thing, an indication of warmth, caring and other positive social attributes. But at a more fundamental level, it is construed negatively, as showing a lack of the even more highly valued and masculine-typed attributes of self-control and rationality. Thus, she argues, women are caught in a culturally constructed dilemma: failure to express emotions is regarded as an indicator that they do not measure up to what is expected of them as women, while the expression of emotions is taken as evidence for their intellectual inferiority to men.

From the point of view of men, this dilemma is just as coercive and arguably at least as damaging to health and well-being. For men, the expression of emotions is negatively valued and seen as inappropriate, while the failure to express emotions has been demonstrated to be associated with negative effects on both physical and emotional well-being. Thus, men are caught by the demands of cultural prescriptions of masculinity in a situation in which whatever they do will be less than ideal.

Gender differences in the expression of emotion

It is important to distinguish between the experience of emotion and its behavioural and physiological expression. This chapter focuses mainly on the expression of emotion, rather than on self-reports of intensity of feeling, concerning which the evidence is somewhat contradictory. Some reviewers (for example Larson and Pleck 1999) conclude that males and females rate the strength of their emotions approximately equally, while others (for example Kring and Gordon 1998) conclude that men actually experience emotions to a somewhat lesser degree than do women. Differences between studies in methodologies, and the problems of interpreting self-reports of private experiences, make it difficult to draw firm conclusions. Whether gender differences in reports of the subjective experience of emotion actually reflect any underlying difference in experience is impossible to determine.

There is substantial controlled evidence demonstrating that males of all ages have higher levels of control over the expression of most emotions, and a greater degree of difficulty in expressing their emotions openly when the situation requires it; males also spend more time than females ruminating over negative emotions (for example McConatha *et al.* 1994), suggesting that controlling and inhibiting the expression of emotion may have negative conseqeunces.

The evidence that men, generally, express their emotions less often, less openly and with less amplitude than do women is quite strong (Brody 1999). Men share their emotions with fewer people than do women, often only with their female partners (Rime *et al.* 1992). Men also express emotions with less intensity than do women, and their behaviour seems less affected by their reported levels of emotions than is women's (Barrett *et al.* 1998). However, the level of emotional expression is not a simple matter of gender, but is complexly determined by the nature of the emotion, the situation, the presence of various categories of other person, and the individual's history (Brody 1999). It seems probable, however, that a history of the inhibition of emotional expression, and a perception that a 'real man' should be unemotional, are likely to affect men's self-reports of emotion in ways that make direct comparisons with women's self-reports somewhat problematic.

Most contemporary researchers and theorists agree that gender differences in emotional expression do not spring from any essential, biological difference between men and women but from cultural expectations, social roles and childhood socialization (Fischer 1993; Lupton 1998; Brody 1999; Larson and Pleck 1999). Brody (1999) has reviewed literature to demonstrate that biological differences between men and women are of very little relevance in the expression of emotions. Rather, she argues, differences in the expression of emotions are explained largely by the different social roles occupied by men and women: men are encouraged not to express vulnerability or warmth as it reduces their ability to fulfil the provider role and to compete with other men. Larson and Pleck (1999), on the basis of a review of evidence on men's expressiveness, have reached a similar conclusion. They argue that everyday life traditionally exposes men to situations which elicit different emotions from those experienced by women. Thus, while men and women are capable of the same ranges of emotions, men are more likely to experience frustration or anger in their working lives and to have fewer opportunities for positive emotional experiences with children and other family members.

It is important to distinguish between cultural stereotypes that prescribe that men should be unemotional, and the actual behaviours of men. Social stereotypes lead to a widespread belief that men both experience and express most emotions to a lesser degree than do women (for example Plant *et al.* 2000). Such stereotypes have been demonstrated to influence observers' interpretations of men's and women's behaviour (Robinson and Johnson 1997; Plant *et al.* 2000). Thus, cultural stereotypes are exaggerations or caricatures of actual gender differences in emotional expression, but the fact that they exist and are widely internalized means that they tend to reinforce and amplify socially transmitted differences.

Lucas and Gohm (2000), summarizing research from several large-scale international surveys, concluded that there was some evidence for a slightly lesser tendency among men to express negative emotions, particularly the internally focused emotions of fear and sadness, but that these differences are small and, for some emotions at least, rather inconsistent. Research is, however, consistent in showing that boys and men express at least some emotions to a considerably lesser degree than do girls and women. Mirowsky and Ross (1995), for example, found that men reported experiencing negative feelings less often than women. However, they also found that men reported feeling less free in the expression of emotions than women, suggesting that men may be more likely to under-report the experience of emotion, as one way of dealing with the social imperative to appear unemotional. Kring and Gordon (1998) found that male and female students reported experiencing the same levels of emotion when watching films, but men were less expressive and showed somewhat different patterns of physiological response, again suggesting that the relationship between experience and expression is affected by gender.

Men and women live in different worlds, in terms of the expression of emotion. There is good evidence from naturalistic research studies (for example Goldshmidt and Weller 2000) that men use emotional language and 'emotion' words significantly less often than do women. Gender differences in emotional expressiveness are transmitted to children in the first instance by their parents and caregivers (Lupton 1998). Parents react differently to boy babies and to girl babies, so that girls become more socially reactive and boys more physically active from an early age. From early childhood, boys are exposed to fewer emotion-oriented conversations with parents and peers, and are not encouraged to express emotions verbally (for example Adams et al. 1995; Fivush et al. 2000). Boys, and men, thus learn to inhibit the expression of emotion. Different patterns of verbal and overt behaviour then lead to different patterns of reactions by parents and later by peers and other adults. Thus, divergent trajectories are established during infancy in emotional expression, as in many other aspects of behaviour, and the interactive nature of social expression means that male and female children become increasingly different as they develop, in emotion as in other aspects of social behaviour (Brody 1999).

The argument that differences in emotional expressiveness between boys and girls are socially, rather than biologically, caused is also supported by evidence (Brody 1997) that children whose fathers have taken an involved and non-traditional approach to fatherhood show lower levels of gender stereotyping in their emotional expression than do children whose fathers are more traditional in their attitudes and behaviours. Chapter 8 discusses the roles of fathers, and the benefits to men, their partners and their children, of non-traditional approaches to fathering in more depth.

It is notable that the debate on gender and the expression of emotions has generally focused on a relative small range of emotions. The expression of depression, sadness and grief is seen as particularly feminine, as is the expression of tenderness. Women are also expected to express positive emotions more openly and flamboyantly than are men.

But, as Lupton (1998) has pointed out, the stereotype that men are, and should be, unemotional does not appear to apply to some emotions. Women are less reluctant than men to express negative emotions such as fear, sadness or disappointment, while men are more willing to express emotions which reflect power and which are likely to be perceived as demonstrating control (Timmers *et al.* 1998). In particular, anger and jealousy are considered appropriate for men and inappropriate for women. These differences are found not only in actual behaviour but also in commonly held stereotypes about men and women (Plant *et al.* 2000); men are believed to be more likely to experience anger and pride, but less likely to experience sadness, fear or depression. These stereotypes are found even among quite young children (Karbon *et al.* 1992), indicating the pervasiveness of this cultural belief.

Men, in fact, are positively encouraged to be overcome by jealous rage (Lupton 1998), particularly if their possessions, their social status, or their exclusive sexual relationship with a woman is threatened. Emotional reactions in these instances, especially if they involve aggressive and irrational behaviour, are seen as entirely appropriate for a traditional man. The evidence on the actual expression of negative externally focused emotions such as jealousy and anger by men and women provides a counterpoint to that on the expression of negative internally focused emotions: it appears that men and women experience anger and jealousy to about the same degree, but men are more likely to express these emotions. For example, both men (Buss and Perry 1992) and boys (Buntaine and Costenbader 1997) report levels of anger which are equal to those of girls and women, but exhibit more aggressive behaviours.

The argument that men are evolutionarily and physiologically predisposed to experience sexual jealousy, and thus that destructive behaviour such as partner violence is both inevitable and excusable, has been most strongly propounded in Buss's (2000) specific innate modular theory. Research such as that of Buss *et al.* (1992) has shown that men tend to respond emotionally and physiologically more strongly than women to imagined scenarios in which a partner becomes sexually involved with someone else. Buss (2000) and others have interpreted this and other research as evidence for an underlying, evolutionarily determined biological difference between men and women in the capacity to experience jealousy.

However, several researchers (for example Grice and Seely 2000; Harris 2000) have failed to replicate these findings. Harris (2000) demonstrated that men show greater reactivity than women to imagined scenarios involving sexual activity of any kind, and thus that the effect was specific to sexuality and not jealousy. Other researchers (for example DeSteno and Salovey 1996; Hupka and Bank 1996) have also criticized this evolutionary model, arguing on the basis of survey research that individual differences in jealousy are better explained by the social construction of gender roles, and in particular by socially mediated gender differences in beliefs about the relationships between sexual activity, emotional closeness, love and betrayal, than they are by biological sex.

Further, Pines and Friedman (1998) failed to find any differences between men and women in reports of the experience of jealousy, but did find that men are more likely than women to express jealousy verbally or through overt behaviours. This difference in behaviour, despite no apparent difference in the experience of the emotion, may once more be explained by cultural beliefs about gender and emotion. There is some evidence for a strong cultural influence on such attitudes and beliefs. Delgado *et al.* (1997) compared Spanish and British attitudes to jealousy and violent behaviour, and showed that Spaniards, both male and female, were likely to regard sexual jealousy as an uncontrollable emotion among men (although not among women) and an adequate excuse for violent criminal assault against female partners. The effect was considerably smaller among British respondents, supporting the view that this attitude about men's inability to deal with at least some emotions has cultural rather than biological roots. There is also evidence from several cultures to show that men who are violent to their female partners report higher levels of jealousy than other men (Dutton *et al.* 1996; Holtzworth-Munroe *et al.* 1997; Russell and Wells 2000).

In summary, there are emotions which appear to run counter to the unemotional man stereotype, but they are emotions which are detrimental to men's relationships with their families, and to the emotional well-being of men themselves. Men, it seems, are allowed to show emotions, but only those which are bad for them and the people about whom they care.

There is a large experimental literature on the effects of emotional expression on health, which in general demonstrates that the expression of emotional experience has a positive effect on emotional well-being, physical health and immune functions (Smyth 1998; Brody 1999). Pennebaker (1993), for example, has demonstrated that emotional self-expression through writing diaries produces beneficial changes in immune functioning. A review of experimental research of this type concluded that written emotional expression led to significant improvements in physical health, psychological well-being, physiological functioning and general day-to-day functioning, but did not appear to affect health behaviours (Smyth 1998).

Exactly how the expression of emotions benefits health is not entirely clear. It has been argued that the effect may occur as a result of the positive social interactions which arise as a result of the sharing of emotions; however, Pennebaker (1997) has demonstrated measurable benefits on immune functioning even when research participants simply typed emotional material into word processor files which were then deleted unread. Thus, it would appear that the mere expression of emotional material (an activity which men are taught to avoid) is enough to have measurable benefits on well-being.

Gender and emotional help-seeking

There is evidence that men cope less well than women with major life events: men, for example, have elevated levels of suicide during marital separation (Cantor and Slater 1995) or bereavement (Li 1995) while women do not. Such research suggests that men have fewer personal and social resources for coping emotionally with negative life events, and it has been argued that men's socially mediated difficulty in expressing their emotions or making use of emotional support may go some way to explaining this difficulty.

As was pointed out in Chapter 2, men make less use than women of psychological services (Jorm 1994). This difference has been explained in terms of the stigma attached to help-seeking for men (Levant 1996) as well as by the possibility that counselling theories and methods are more appropriate for traditionally feminine than for traditionally masculine individuals (Philipson 1993). Client surveys (Bugge *et al.* 1985; Henderson and Lyddon 1997) show that men who do use psychological services are generally less satisfied than women with those services, and rate therapists less positively, suggesting that even when men do seek help, they may not be getting what they want.

The arguments presented in this chapter would suggest that men's relative reluctance to seek counselling for emotional problems can be seen as stemming from a culturally based reluctance to discuss their emotions openly, and a sense that a man who needs to ask for help has failed in one of the fundamental tasks of successful male adulthood. However, the identification of harmful cultural practices does not in itself provide a solution to the problem, and may in fact lead to a victim-blaming approach by which men are criticized for the mismatch between the cultural expectations placed on men and the nature of psychological services. At one level, the solution to this problem may lie in the raising of boys and men who feel comfortable expressing their emotions and are who able to seek help when it will be useful. But at the same time, the nature of that help needs to be considered.

On this issue, some researchers (for example Silverberg 1984) have taken the view that there is a need to develop counselling methods which are appropriate for uncommunicative people who find it difficult to allow another person to control or dominate any social interaction. Others (for example Erickson 1993) have argued that therapists can be most useful if they develop strategies to help men to challenge traditional concepts of masculinity and to apply feminist principles in their lives. It is frequently argued that contemporary counselling theory and practice, with its emphasis on sharing and trust, is fundamentally more appropriate for women than for men, particularly for those who have internalized traditional views of appropriate masculine behaviour.

Male socialization, it is argued (Granello 2000), has a restrictive effect on men's ability to explore their emotions and thus to benefit from psychotherapy. Men's conversational styles, for example, seem less appropriate than women's to the close and detailed verbal exchanges expected by many therapists (Werner-Wilson *et al.* 1997). Femiano (1992) has also argued that many nonverbal techniques which are widely used in therapy, and which are generally regarded as unquestionably useful, can create difficulties for some men. The use of relaxation, for example, requires clients to relinquish at least some control and to place themselves in a position of vulnerability. While this and other techniques may enable some men to learn to explore their emotions more openly, for others it may be too much of a challenge at a time when they are already facing emotional challenges.

Whether the solution to this problem lies in changing methods to make them more acceptable to traditional men, or in developing strategies to help men feel more comfortable with the sharing of emotions, mainstream psychology has generally failed to consider the gendered nature of its models and techniques, its assumptions about the process of therapy, and the implications for men as clients. Decades ago, Silverberg (1984) was arguing that traditional psychotherapy, with its aim on the exploration of feelings and achieving of insight, was inappropriate for many men. He argued that men, particularly traditional men, would feel more comfortable with action- and behaviour-oriented approaches, with an emphasis on the rational and impersonal definition and analysis of the problem under discussion.

It is important, however, to acknowledge that not all men are incapable of discussing their emotions and admitting vulnerability. The development of traditional male-oriented models of therapeutic process is not necessarily the most appropriate response to the issues that exist for men and therapy, and the implicit assumption that therapists can best help men by developing techniques which reinforce emotional inexpressiveness may, in the long run, disadvantage men.

Feminist therapists (Slive 1986; Ganley 1988; Erickson 1993) have put the view that uncritical acceptance of stereotypic and essentialist notions of what will or will not be appropriate for male clients is likely to be less beneficial to men than the confrontation and questioning of traditionally masculine and problematic strategies of coping with emotion. It is obviously not the case that men are incapable of benefiting from counselling as it is presently practised. Nahon and Lander (1992), for example, described a counselling clinic for recently separated men which used traditional counselling methods that focused on the exploration of emotion. Separated men were not, as expected, unwilling to seek help, and were described as readily participating in discussions of emotion and adjustment which they found beneficial.

It may be that counselling is most useful if it helps men to recognize and challenge gendered aspects of lifestyles, attitudes and expectations that contribute to emotional distress and to personal and family difficulties. Men may benefit from 'consciousness raising', the exploration of ways in which the social construction of gender restricts their choices and behaviours. Some groups of men may find it easier than others to adapt to modes of therapy which have generally been more appropriate for women, whether the traditional 'talking cure' or a feminist approach emphasizing an awareness of gender roles.

The literature on the specific needs of particular groups has tended to focus on two groups of men who face considerable, although different, levels of stigmatization: black men and homosexual men. The literature on black men and their counselling needs derives mainly from the USA, and identifies African American men as a group who are likely to benefit from an approach which is particular sensitive to their subjectivities, their often difficult and stigmatized social position, and their sense of alienation from mainstream American values (Lee 1990). African American men appear to be at higher risk than men from at least some other ethnic backgrounds for emotional disturbance. This, it is argued, arises from entrenched and continuing racism which places additional stressors on them at personal, social and economic levels (Thorn and Sarata 1998). Such men may find mainstream therapeutic techniques of limited value. Larrabee (1986) has stressed the importance of affirming the value of these men's view of themselves and the world, particularly when they have not made an individual decision to seek counselling but are undergoing therapy as part of a court order or other legal proceedings. However, evidence on counselling needs of African American men is scarce, and that on the needs of other stigmatized groups almost completely nonexistent.

Particular issues also arise with gay men who seek therapy, and therapists need to understand the issues which these men are likely to confront (Purcell *et al.* 1996). Several authors (for example Graham *et al.* 1984) have pointed out that many therapists feel that they lack the skills and knowledge necessary to work with men who are in same-sex relationships, while surveys (for example Garnets *et al.* 1991) have demonstrated considerable variability in heterosexual therapists' ability or willingness to deal sympathetically with gay clients.

There exists a considerable literature on counselling with gay men, stressing the particular issues which arise for this group, such as the development and maintenance of a positive self-identity in a homophobic and hostile society, dealing with anti-gay attitudes and violence, and developing strategies for coping with HIV and other sexually transmitted diseases (Shannon and Woods 1991; Dunkle 1994) as well as issues such as relationships and sexual problems which are common to many individuals seeking psychological help, regardless of their gender or sexual orientation (Ussher 1990). It might be expected that gay men could be more willing to share emotions and more responsive to verbal counselling strategies, but it is important with this group, as with any other group of men, to avoid stereotyping and to recognize diversity.

It is possible, however, that there needs to be a radical realignment of counselling theory and methods in order to come to grips with men's traditional ways of seeing the world and their preferred ways of seeking help. The question of whether therapies need to change radically, or whether they need to incorporate techniques to increase men's level of comfort with traditional change methods, remains an open one, and there is an obvious need for continuing research in this area. Research on psychological distress and its alleviation has frequently concentrated on women. Caverhill (1997), for example, has pointed out that men and women grieve for the loss of their partners in quite different ways, but that most bereavement research is done with widows rather than widowers, and called for efforts to understand the special needs of bereaved men.

Conclusion

In summary, then, there is a need for a greater focus in theory and research on the particular counselling needs of men, which have been largely neglected in the practical and theoretical literature. But at a more fundamental level, this chapter suggests that there is a need for a greater awareness of the gendered nature of emotional expression across all settings, and the difficulties which this can cause for men.

Summary

- Cultural stereotypes demand that a 'real' man should express emotions to a lesser extent than do women, although the stereotype of the 'unemotional man' applies most strongly to negative internally focused emotions and those which show vulnerability. Some emotions, such as anger and jealousy, are actually seen as more appropriate for men than for women.
- The subjective nature of emotional experience means that it is impossible to assess gender differences in subjective experience. But there is evidence that men in general express emotions to a lesser degree than women, and that this difference is transmitted socially, by parents, peers and the media.
- The expression of emotion has been demonstrated to be beneficial to physical and emotional health, and individuals who find the expression of emotion difficult may experience negative outcomes; gender differences in emotional expression mean that men are less likely to be able to benefit from emotional expression than are women.
- Men are less likely than women to seek professional counselling or therapy for emotional problems, and those who do are less satified with the services they receive, than are women.
- Mainstream counselling and psychotherapeutic techniques that rely on verbal expression of emotion, admission of vulnerability, or relinquishment of control through relaxation or hypnosis may be more appropriate for women than for men.
- Commentators disagree as to whether the mismatch between therapeutic techniques and men's needs is better addressed through the development of radically different therapies or through the development of strategies to help men feel comfortable with emotional expression.

◆ While there is some research that explores therapeutic appropraches which are appropriate for some specific groups of men, there remains a need for considerably more attention to be paid to addressing theory and technique which can benefit all men, regardless of their particular circumstances.

Additional reading

Brody, L.R. (1999) *Gender, Emotion and the Family*. Cambridge, MA: Harvard University Press.
Lupton, D. (1998) *The Emotional Self: A Sociocultural Exploration*. London: Sage.

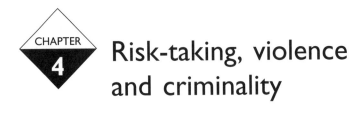

Risk-taking, violence and criminality

Chapter 2 indicated that men have a shorter life expectancy than do women, and pointed to differences in health behaviours and health service use which might go some way to explaining this difference. It is, however, notable that the major sex differences in death rates are not in the most common causes of death, coronary heart disease and cancer, but in accidents and violence. This chapter explores the ways in which hegemonic models of masculinity encourage men to take physical risks and to expose themselves to danger in everyday life, in occupational choice, in transport choices and in sporting activities. The social prescription that young men must 'prove themselves' by taking unnecessary risks, and the positioning of caution and concern for safety as feminine and inferior, lead young men to behave in self-destructive ways.

The chapter also explores the gendered nature of crime. Men are many times more likely than women to be both perpetrators and victims of crime, particularly violent crime, and it has been hypothesized that violence and criminality are strategies by which men can enact hegemonic gender roles when other strategies are unavailable to them. The growing proportion of men who are unable to share the benefits of patriarchy are those who are most likely to turn to violence and criminal strategies for expressing traditional masculinity.

Accidental injuries

Injuries represent one of the leading causes of death and disability throughout the world. They constitute a significant public health problem, at least in part because they affect people in their young and middle years (Krug *et al.* 2000). However, their impact has tended to be underestimated, and the study of accidental injury from an epidemiological perspective has been limited. Language and social discourse construct accidental injuries as isolated incidents, rather than as the result of socially sanctioned patterns of behaviour. Injuries are construed as resulting from individual faults in the victim – carelessness in the case of accidental injury, criminal personality or social deviance in the case of deliberate criminal violence. There is little analysis of the physical and social circumstances that are associated with high levels of accidental injury in particular social groups; there is in fact surprisingly little awareness that injury rates show strong gender differences, with men having several times the rate of accident-related injury and death as women.

As Courtenay (1998) has argued, young men in particular are encouraged to engage in risky behaviours that put them at high risk of injury and death, but their health has not in general been seen as a high priority by public health officials. It is notable, though, that in the USA, the male–female mortality discrepancy peaks dramatically between the ages of 15 and 35, supporting the view that it is not diseases of old age but behavioural factors, especially high-risk activities, that are responsible for a major part in the discrepancy in life expectancy (Smith 1993).

This chapter argues that accidental injury occurs in a gendered social context. It is necessary to understand men's excess rates of accidental injury in terms other than that of individual men choosing freely to engage in risky activities. Nor is it at all useful to ascribe young men's risk-taking to biological imperatives: the ascription of unwise behaviour to 'testosterone poisoning', and the use of dubious analogies with the instinctive behaviour patterns of some other species, serve to deny the role of social influences in young men's behaviour (Fletcher 1997).

Gender differences in risk of accidental injury or death are demonstrated even in early childhood. An Australian study (Lam et al. 1999) showed that boys were twice as likely as girls to die in play-related accidents, while a US survey (Stone et al. 2000) found that boys were twice as likely as girls to be injured or killed by falling from windows. In Argentina, Murgio et al. (1999) found that boys were twice as likely as girls to suffer head injuries requiring treatment. Danseco et al. (2000) analysed national US data on medically treated childhood injuries, and found that boys were, overall, one and a half times as likely as girls to be injured, and twice as likely to die from injuries.

These epidemiological patterns in childhood reflect gendered differences in injury rates throughout adult life. Males in general are around three times as likely to die from injuries than are females (Li and Baker 1996). The Australian Bureau of Statistics (1996a) has demonstrated that the death rate for men is several times that for women for motor-vehicle accidents, drownings and all other external causes of death, except falls (elderly women are the group who are most likely to die as the result of falls, because of their high risk of major fractures).

Death rates are generally paralleled by rates of morbidity, hospitalization and disability. Evidence from several countries shows that men are between two and five times as likely as women to be admitted to hospital as a result of injuries of all kinds. For example, Gardiner *et al.* (2000) found that 75 per cent of intensive care admissions in Auckland were men and boys. Watson and Ozanne-Smith (2000) in Victoria, Australia, showed that 62 per cent of all medically recorded injuries, including three-quarters of all fatal injuries, were sustained by males. An analysis by age group showed that injury-related hospitalization rates were higher for men than for women in all age groups up to 64 years of age, although they were slightly lower above that age (Li and Ozanne-Smith 2000).

Men are significantly more likely than women to experience non-fatal fractures; for example, a Swedish study found men more likely than women to sustain fractures to the clavicle, generally as a result of bicycling or sporting accidents (Nowak *et al.* 2000). This effect is found throughout childhood and most of adult life, reversing only in old age when the endocrine changes associated with ageing in women leads to a high rate of osteoporosis among older women.

Males are also three to four times as likely as females to experience spinal cord injuries, and their injuries tend to be more severe, meaning they are likely to experience greater levels of disability over a longer period of time (Nobunaga *et al.* 1999; van Asbeck *et al.* 2000). Kolakowsky-Hayner *et al.* (1999), confirming that the majority of spinal cord and traumatic brain injury patients were young men, also found that most were heavy drinkers, supporting the view that it is an interaction between traditionally male-typed health behaviours and traditionally male recreational and sporting activities which places individuals at risk of traumatic spinal injury.

The excess of men in accidental injury and death is observable both in broad terms and when one focuses on any of occupational, traffic-related or recreational circumstances. An interesting pattern, however, is observable across all three of these areas; social expectations and gender-based assumptions mean that men are over-represented in dangerous occupations and leisure activities. In each area of activity, men's higher rates of injury are explicable not by individual men's carelessness but by men's higher exposure to risk. When one accounts for gender differences in exposure, by controlling for male–female differences in participation in manual and construction-related occupations, male–female differences in time and distance travelled in traffic and male–female differences in participation in active sports, the differences disappear. What this suggests is that it is not the risk behaviours of individual men that require understanding, but the social forces which lead to the gender differences in choice of occupation and of recreational activity.

Work-related serious injuries and deaths are significantly more common among men than women. Caradoc-Davies and Hawker (1997) have used New Zealand data to estimate the rate of work-related injury for men to be twice that for women. This is particularly observable in physically demanding and hazardous occupations which are characterized by a high preponderance of male workers. For example, a Welsh study showed that men suffered eleven times as many work-related burns as women; more specifically, it was young men in physical occupations who were at highest risk (Munnoch *et al.* 2000). In the USA, men are several times as likely as women to be injured by farm machinery (Gerberich *et al.* 1998) or in factory work (Wong *et al.* 1998).

But these gender differences are almost entirely explained by differences in men's and women's involvement in high-risk occupations. In fact, several studies have shown that, when differential rates of involvement between men and women are taken into account, women are actually more likely to be injured or killed in manufacturing or other high-risk occupations than are men (Sahl *et al.* 1997; Hansen and Jensen 1998; Ore 1998; Palsson *et al.* 1998).

The armed forces are the occupational group which is perhaps most stereotypically and traditionally male, most identified with hegemonic masculinity, and with concepts which equate maleness with aggression, and physical violence with superiority (Petersen 1998). It is also an occupational group with a very high rate of accidental injury and death (Anonymous 1999). Yet, while the armed forces are overwhelmingly male, female army personnel are proportionally twice as likely as male personnel to be injured (for example Snedecor *et al.* 2000). The impact of lifestyle and behaviour, rather than an individual's sex *per se*, is illustrated in an analysis of motor-vehicle accidents among US Army personnel (Bell *et al.* 2000) which showed that male and female personnel had equal rates of motor-vehicle-related accidents and injury. In this group, motor vehicle accidents were not predicted by sex, but by younger age, a pattern of heavy drinking and a habitual failure to use seat belts. This suggests that it is the adoption of a particular lifestyle involving risk-taking and other behaviours typical of young men which places individuals at risk of injury.

In the general population, there is consistent evidence that men are more likely to experience traffic-related accidents than women. For example, men are three times as likely as women to be killed in motor-vehicle accidents (Li *et al.* 1998) and have several times the rate of women of injury or death in bicycle accidents (for example Li and Baker 1996; Welander *et al.* 1999). But again these observed differences are almost entirely explained by gender differences in exposure to risk, such as time spent travelling, distance travelled and use of bicycles by men and women (Li and Baker 1996; Li *et al.* 1998). Even among over-65s, men are twice as likely as women to be killed in motor-vehicle accidents (Stevens *et al.* 1999) but again the difference disappears when death rates are adjusted to take into account the gender differences in time and distance travelled (Lourens *et al.* 1999).

The same pattern can be seen in the case of sporting and recreational injuries. Sporting injuries and fatal accidents are also more common among boys and men than among girls and women (for example Williams *et al.* 1998). But once again, this effect is entirely explained by higher levels of sporting involvement among males. In fact, girls and women who do play competitive sport are consistently shown to be more prone to musculo-skeletal injury than boys and men (Stevenson *et al.* 1998; Hosea *et al.* 2000; Powell and Barber-Foss 2000).

Thus, although social discourses frequently hold that men are somehow biologically driven to behave carelessly and to risk death, often through inappropriate analogies with other animal species in which males struggle physically among themselves for status, findings such as these support the view that differences in male and female accidental death rates are explained by social and cultural factors which encourage boys to choose activities which expose them to greater risks.

These factors are strongly embedded in hegemonic and traditional views of the ideal male as tough and physical, as hard-working, and as unconcerned about his own safety and well-being, and in cultural constructions which regard these characteristics as superior and advantageous despite their obvious capacity to harm (Petersen 1998). Boys are socialized from an early age to expose themselves to risk; for example, Morrongiello and Dawber (2000) showed that mothers of small girls were more likely to caution their daughters against potentially risky activities, while mothers of small boys encouraged them to take risks. Hillier and Morrongiello (1998) found that primary school age boys perceived a range of play activities as less risky than did girls, and differences in risk-taking behaviour could be predicted from beliefs about risk and causality of injury (Morrongiello and Rennie 1998). What this suggests is that young men grow up without being taught how to recognize and avoid physical danger; cultural discourses and expectations then make it likely that they will choose to engage in activities which place them at risk of injury, which in turn places them at high risk of permanent disablement or preventable death. Yet analyses of men's risk behaviours tend to focus on the individual and to ascribe risky choices to individual foolishness, rather than seeing young men as victims of social and media pressure. This lack of attention to the social pressures on young men can be contrasted with the focus on social influences on young women's behaviour, for example in the area of disordered eating (for example Fallon *et al.* 1994). It seems acceptable to position young women as the victims of social forces, while parallel arguments surrounding risk patterns in young men are almost entirely absent from the political and public-health agenda.

Crimes of violence

The foregoing section of this chapter has argued for a need for more attention to be paid to the risk of accidental injury and death among men, and particularly young men. The view that young men should be treated as victims of social, media and cultural stereotypes, rather than as stupid or foolhardy, is one which has been neglected to a surprising degree. However, it is consistent with broader models of public health which acknowledge the ways in which structural factors constrain individual choice. It is consistent, for example, with views that see tobacco advertising as influential in young people's decisions to smoke, and media images as influential in young women's concerns about their body shape. Physical risk-taking, like smoking and unhealthy eating, is an individual choice but it is one which is made in a specific cultural context and with particular social and personal consequences. The argument presented in the section of this chapter is consistent with contemporary assumptions in the field of public health.

When one turns to another category of activity that places young men disproportionately at risk of injury, disability or death, however, a sympathetic point of view which places the young man's choices within a social context is likely to meet with some resistance. The male nature of crime is readily demonstrated. An Australian report compiled from police reports (Mukherjee et al. 1997), for example, indicated that men vastly outnumber women as perpetrators of every category of crime, with the gender difference being strongest for crimes of violence, where the difference is approximately tenfold. While male gender roles can be implicated as causal factors in criminality (for example Messerschmidt 1993), men who commit crimes are not generally seen as the victims of social pressures but as individually responsible for their choices; the impacts of traditional social expectations of men's behaviour are largely ignored.

The effects of criminal activity on men's health are exacerbated by the risk of imprisonment. The evidence that imprisonment has negative effects on prisoners' physical health, emotional well-being, social position and likelihood of avoiding future criminal activity, is overwhelming (Weisbuch 1991; Marquart et al. 1996) but the specific details of that literature are outside the scope of this chapter. Clearly prison is extremely bad for the prisoner's health, and prisons are overwhelmingly male institutions. In Australia in 1994, for example, 95 per cent of all incarcerated adults were men (Australian Bureau of Statistics 1996b).

The male–female difference in perpetration of crime is most evident in the category of physical assault, but is also strongly apparent in the most violent of all crimes, murder. In this area, the literature distinguishes between 'non-intimate' and 'intimate' homicide. Intimate homicides, the murder of a current or former relationship partner, show quite different characteristics and predictors from non-intimate homicides.

Non-intimate homicides are more common, for example accounting for approximately 75 per cent of all murders in Australia (Carach and James 1998). Men are about three times as likely as women to be either the victims (Pratt and Deosaransingh 1997) or the perpetrators (Carach and

James 1998) of non-intimate homicides. While men are also three or four times as likely as women to be the perpetrators of intimate homicides (Carach and James 1998; Easteal 1993), the victims of these crimes are most likely to be women (Carach and James surveyed intimate homicides in Australia and found that 77 per cent involved a man killing a woman, 21 per cent a woman killing a man and 2 per cent a man killing another man). While these are Australian data, and population-based murder rates differ considerably between countries – six times as high in the USA as in England, for example (National Campaign Against Violence and Crime 1998) – the gender ratios among both perpetrators and victims remain relatively constant.

Considering other violent crimes, such as assault, it is notable that psychological research has focused almost exclusively on domestic assault, and has ignored assault outside the family. This is despite the fact that assault by an acquaintance or stranger in a public place is the most common form of assault reported to the police (Victoria Police 1997); such assaults are overwhelming perpetrated by young men against other young men. By contrast, incidents of family violence reported to the police are almost entirely perpetrated by men against women (Victoria Police 1997). It is important to stress that the increased public and systemic awareness of violence against women is important in terms of social equity and public health. In discussing the gendered nature of violent assault against men, it is of course important not to minimize the impacts of violence and abuse against women. A feminist approach to the psychology of men's health, however, does not attempt to argue that men's needs must be greater than women's, or that women's experiences are any less legitimate than those of men. Rather, it recognizes that both men and women live in a gendered social context, and that men and women have equally legitimate, though different, needs that can usefully be explored from a gendered perspective.

Attention has been placed on the reluctance of law enforcement systems to treat family violence as serious criminal assault (Office of the Status of Women 1995) and feminists have been influential in changing cultural attitudes to family crime in ways which benefit vulnerable women and children. It is also the case that law enforcement officers may hold attitudes that construct violent assault between young men as a private or trivial matter, or as normal social behaviour in certain circumstances and locations. Thus, young men may internalize a view that violent crime and victimization are normal aspects of masculine life.

As has been demonstrated, gender is the strongest predictor of criminal involvement, but the masculine gender role has not been studied seriously as an explanation for crime. Rather, Messerschmidt (1993) has argued that social research has responded to the masculine nature of crime by paying attention to what it is that makes women relatively law-abiding, rather than focusing on why men commit crimes. While this focus reinforces the notion of men as 'normal' human beings and women as the 'other', it fails to address the gendered experiences of men that lead to crime. In Messerschmidt's view, crime is a social practice that has as its aim the accomplishment of masculinity, and it is adopted when other resources are unavailable. According to this view, men who have internalized hegemonic models of appropriate masculine behaviour commit crimes if they are unable to enact the traditional masculine gender roles to which they aspire in socially acceptable ways, such as obtaining paid employment or establishing and providing for a family. The well-documented associations between crime, unemployment, poverty and social deprivation (for example Farrington 1998; Kawachi et al. 1999) support this social explanation of crime. Once again, explanations for men's greater risk are to be found not in individual foolishness or in essential biological characteristics. Rather, it arises from a combination of material conditions which provide few alternatives, and social imperatives which restrict men's abilities to construct satisfying lives for themselves outside the expectations of patriarchy.

Men as victims of crime

As well as being more likely to experience accidental injury and to commit crimes of violence, men also appear to be more likely than women to be the victims of assault. For example, Wladis et al. (1999), in Sweden, found that men were three times as likely as women to be admitted to hospital as a result of physical assault. It seems that the same factors which may predispose men to crime are those which place them at risk of criminal victimization.

Despite evidence for high levels of physical assault against men, media, police, the education system and other institutions concentrate their efforts to promote the avoidance of crime among women. Women are enjoined to stay inside at night, to avoid potentially dangerous situations, and to modify their appearance and behaviour in order to avoid becoming victims of crime. No such messages are conveyed to men. In fact, violence between men is normalized. At the time of writing, for example, an Australian state government instrumentality is running a media campaign against domestic violence. Posters feature popular (male) rugby league players with statements such as, 'Hit a woman? That's a crime.' The clear implication is that hitting a *man* is *not* a crime, but a normal and indeed positively valued activity. It is thus unsurprising that young men are less likely than young women to behave in ways that prevent their becoming victims of violent crime (Hammig and Moranetz 2000). Men are far more likely than women to be murdered by a stranger or in a public place (Pratt and Deosaransingh 1997), suggesting that there is a need for men to be taught strategies for avoiding victimization in public situations.

Men are also more likely than women to be revictimized. A US study (Cooper *et al.* 2000) demonstrated that the victims of violence who were most at risk of revictimization were unemployed men, members of minorities, and involved with illicit drugs. This suggests that particular lifestyle choices, which are likely to be adopted by men who have few other alternatives, not only predispose towards criminal activity but also predispose to becoming a victim of repeated violence.

Again, blaming the individual may be less useful than examining the underlying social structures. The finding, for example, that in the USA boys aged under 5 are twice as likely to be murdered as girls (Collins and Nichols 1999) can hardly be attributed to those small children's individual risky choices, but must be seen in the context of the children's lives and the behaviours and assumptions of the adults around them.

Suicide

Perhaps the most distressing aspect of men's higher involvement in risk-taking and lower rates of self-protective behaviours is the high rate of suicide among men. Suicide is more common among males than among females at all age groups in all western countries. Lee *et al.* (1999) showed that suicide in US children and adolescents is four times as common among males as among females. Among adults in western societies, males also commit suicide at around four times the rate of females (Taylor *et al.* 1998; Yip 1998).

Interestingly, this gender difference does not appear to obtain in Asian countries. Yip (1998) demonstrated that male and female suicide rates were roughly equal in Hong Kong, while in China, the rate is actually somewhat lower for men than for women (Yip *et al.* 2000), again suggesting that explanations are to be found in social and cultural factors rather than in anything innately self-destructive about men.

The evidence supports the view that it is marginalized men, men who are denied the benefits of an inequitable patriarchal system, who are at highest risk of suicide. Lee *et al.* (1999) showed that suicide rates are highest among migrant, indigenous, gay and other minority men. Marginalization, poverty and social isolation appear to affect men more strongly and negatively than they do women. For example, Taylor *et al.* (1998) have demonstrated that low socio-economic status is a more important predictor of suicide for men than for women, suggesting that women may be better able to draw on other resources when their economic resources are limited. Similarly, loss of a partner affects men more negatively than women. In the USA, divorced men have twice the suicide rate of married men, while there is no difference for women (Kposowa 2000). In Hong Kong, where there is no consistent gender difference in suicide rates, elderly single or widowed men are at increased risk (Yip *et al.* 1998).

Alcohol consumption is strongly associated with both suicide and homicide (Lester 1995). Woods *et al.* (1997) surveyed US teenagers and showed that suicide attempts tended to cluster with other health-risk behaviours, including use of alcohol and illicit drugs, smoking and fighting. Higher rates of suicide among men, and young men in particular, are related to higher levels of risk-taking more generally (Langhinrichsen-Rohling *et al.* 1998). It is also well established that males and females favour different suicide methods (for example Dudley *et al.* 1998), with males being more likely to use methods which are more immediate and certain, such as shooting, while females use less immediate methods, such as poisoning, which are more readily amenable to discovery and intervention. This difference means that male suicide attempts are more likely to be successful. There are gendered meanings attached to suicide methods, as well as to suicide reasons (killing oneself over a failed relationship, for example, is seen as a feminine thing to do); in particular, unsuccessful suicide attempts are construed as indicative of weakness and femininity (Canetto 1997).

A catastrophic variation on suicide, the murder-suicide, is even more strongly male-typed. Felthous and Hempel (1995), for example, reviewing evidence on murder-suicides in the USA, established that over 95 per cent of perpetrators are male while between 75 and 90 per cent of victims are female. They classify murder-suicides both by the type of psychopathology (depression, sociopathy, psychosis, intoxication, jealousy or paranoia) and by the relationship between perpetrator and victim or victims (partner, child, entire family, adversary, or pseudo-commando and cult). In Australia, Easteal (1994) analysed murder-suicides within adult relationships or ex-relationships. She also concluded that the perpetrators were almost exclusively male, and identified two general categories: an elderly man with a dying or chronically ill wife, motivated by a lack of alternative ways of coping with her illness; and a younger or middle-aged man with an estranged wife, motivated by pathological possessiveness and desire for control.

While these and other researchers have explored typologies of murder-suicide, however, they have failed to address the question of why it is almost exclusively men who commit these crimes. A gendered analysis must take into account the constraints that cultural expectations of masculinity place on men's behaviour. What is it, for example, about men's socialization which can lead to the view that murder and suicide is preferable to an ex-partner choosing how she wants to live her life? While the view that men have a right to control the lives of partners and ex-partners can simply be dismissed as an irrational symptom of psychiatric disorder, to ascribe such behaviour simply to individual pathology does not explain the huge gender difference in its occurrence. There is a need for a sympathetic analysis of the social constraints on men's choices which impel them to behaviours which endanger or destroy their lives and those of their families. More generally, there is a need to explore men's violence in its sociocultural context, to problematize destructive and violent behaviour rather than treating it as normal, unremarkable and natural.

Conclusion

The over-representation of men as victims of accidents and as both victims and perpetrators of crime must be understood in the context of the social constraints on men's behaviour, and not simply in terms of individual choice. The need to conform to social stereotypes of masculinity as involving risk-taking and aggression should be recognized as a major risk factor that influences men's health and reduces their life expectancy.

Summary

◆ Men are at considerably greater risk than women of accidental injury and death, events which comprise a major public health concern throughout the world.
◆ This difference can be explained by gender-based choice of occupational and recreational activities, which place men at greater risk of accidental injury.
◆ Risk-taking and accidental injury do not arise from any essentially male characteristic, but are determined by gender-role socialization which encourages men to seek out specifically risky activities and means that they do not learn to recognize and avoid risk to the same extent as do women.
◆ It is also the case that crimes, and particularly crimes of violence, are predominantly male activities. It can be argued that men turn to crime as a way of enacting hegemonic masculinity, when their social circumstances make it impossible for them to achieve these goals in any more socially acceptable way.
◆ Men are also over-represented as victims of those violent crimes which occur outside the domestic sphere. Men, unlike women, are not taught to recognize and avoid situations in which assault is possible, and criminal assault between men, particularly instances of young men assaulting other young men in sporting or social contexts, is frequently not taken seriously as crime.
◆ Suicide rates among men are several times higher than women in most western countries, although this pattern is not found in Asian countries.
◆ This chapter has argued for a need to explore men's violence and risk-taking from the perspective of gender. It is argued that men are socialized to take risks, and are not trained to recognize physical risk or to take steps to avoid injury or assault.

Additional reading

Krug, E.G., Sharma, G.K. and Lozano, R. (2000) The global burden of injuries, *American Journal of Public Health*, 90: 523–6.
Messerschmidt, J.W. (1993) *Masculinities and Crime: Critique and Reconceptualization of Theory*. Lanham, MD: Rowman & Littlefield.

CHAPTER
5

Sexuality and men's health

We live, there can be no doubt, in a highly sexualized society. Images of sexual activity abound in the media and have since the earliest recorded history; sex, as everybody knows, sells (Thompson 2000). Hand in hand with the high salience of sexuality in society goes a strong differentiation of gender roles with respect to sexual behaviour and attitudes (Blackwood 2000). Indeed, the presence of clearly differentiated gender roles with respect to sexual behaviour is perhaps one of the most consistent of findings across cultures. Gender differences in sexual attitudes and sexual behaviour are widely assumed to be both biologically based and immutable. This chapter argues, however, that many gender differences in attitudes and behaviour pertaining to sex are culturally, rather than biologically, based.

While the precise nature of gender differentiation in sexual attitudes and sexual behaviour, and the extent to which it is enforced by explicit or implicit social rules, varies considerably across societies, there is an almost universal assumption that males have, and should have, more freedom than females in sexual behaviour and expression. It is important, however, to distinguish between cultural assumptions about men's greater sexual freedom and the actual behaviours and attitudes of men. The evidence on this question is more than a little mixed.

Anthropological research into cultural expectations of male and female sexual behaviour has demonstrated that many societies maintain a double standard, with males being permitted substantially higher levels of sexual freedom than females (Barry and Schlegel 1984, 1985). In a survey of 141 societies, Broude and Greene (1976) found that 65 per cent disapproved of premarital sexual behaviour among women to a greater degree than among men. Psychobiologists have attempted to explain such double standards in terms of a hypothesized 'need' to identify correctly a child's biological parents. While identifying the mother is biologically unequivocal, only in a society in which all women were always entirely monogamous could fathers be identified with similar degrees of confidence (a reason, incidentally, why Jewish lineage is carried through the mother rather than the father). This explanation, of course, raises the question of why and to whom the identity of a child's biological father is of interest. Fathering, to a greater extent even than mothering, is a social rather than a biological relationship. The evidence is clear that a 'good father' is one who cares for, and about, his children (Coltrane 1995; Milkie *et al.* 1997); the question of whose genetic material contributed to a child is irrelevant to that relationship. The emphasis placed on the biological relationship is a characteristic of patriarchal societies that regard women and children essentially as the possessions of men rather than as self-determining individuals with equal social status.

In many societies, women are or were unable to own property in their own right, any property becoming their husband's on marriage. In such societies, having several wives becomes a symbol of wealth not only because of the dowries that would have accompanied marriage, but also because the ability to keep several wives would imply that the person possessed sufficient wealth to do so. Of course in societies where the wives themselves become part of a husband's property, having several wives is a direct statement of wealth.

Societal encouragement of male and discouragement of female promiscuity is perhaps illustrated most clearly in considerations of polygamy. In a study of 862 societies, Murdock (1967) reported that while 83 per cent allowed men to have more than one wife, in only four (less than 0.5 per cent) of the societies was it considered acceptable for a woman to have more than one husband. Such patterns represent a formalization of the common observation in western societies that masculinity requires and expects a man to have heterosexual sex with as many women as possible. Popular images and role models perpetuate the equating of masculinity with sexual promiscuity – the 'James Bond' character, envied by men for the extent to which without any effort on his part women offer themselves as sexual partners. Access to a large number of sexual partners is one of the ways in which a man can demonstrate power, wealth and success. The use of the word 'impotence' (literally a lack of power) to refer exclusively to a man's inability to obtain an erection demonstrates the extent to which a man's ability to have penetrative sex is identified with his social and personal power.

These social expectations and stereotypes are not necessarily reflected in the actual behaviours or attitudes of individuals. The extent of gender differences in reported sexual behaviours and attitudes varies greatly, even within superficially similar societies and over relatively short time periods. For example, repeated surveys of sexual behaviours among German university students over 30 years (Schmidt *et al.* 1998) show a marked change in sexual attitudes and behaviours in the late 1960s and early 1970s, but little change since then. Interestingly, it is women's behaviour that appears to have changed: women now begin sexual activity at an earlier age and report more sexual partners than do men, the reverse of the previous pattern. Later initiation of sexual behaviour among males is also the norm in other societies. In New Zealand, Paul *et al.* (2000) found that 32 per cent of girls had had sexual intercourse before the age of 16, compared with 28 per cent of boys. Similarly, Kvalem and Traeen (2000) found that 52 per cent of Norwegian women aged 16 to 20 had had sexual intercourse, compared with 41 per cent of young men.

In other countries, however, males appear more likely to engage in sex at an earlier age. In Hong Kong, male university students were more likely than female students to report that they had engaged in premarital sex, or that they had the intention to do so (Chan and Cheung 1998). In Greece, 27 per cent of males in a national survey of university student reported being virgins, compared with 50 per cent of females (Papadopoulis *et al.* 2000).

Attitudes to sexuality and sexual behaviour also vary between cultures. Overall, 72 per cent of both male and female Greek students endorsed traditional attitudes to sexual behaviour, viewing heterosexual sex within marriage as the most appropriate and desirable pattern of sexual behaviour (Papadopoulis *et al.* 2000). By contrast, even though German students generally restricted their sexual behaviour to a series of monogamous heterosexual relationships, neither male nor female students showed much interest in marriage, and acceptance of the legitimacy of homosexual relationships was high (Schmidt *et al.* 1998).

These varied patterns of behaviour and attitude suggest that cultural and social expectations play a major role in determining men's and women's sexual activities (Blackwood 2000). The concept that promiscuity among men is 'natural' and therefore more socially acceptable than the same behaviour among women, and the view that men have a powerful, almost uncontrollable 'sex drive', have been criticized by feminists who argue that these views are unfounded and are used to benefit men to the detriment of women (for example Dworkin 1997).

Men are popularly although erroneously seen as being unable to control their sexuality, to the extent that offensive, aggressive, violent or even murderous behaviour that has a sexual aspect is at least to some extent viewed as understandable and excusable. Men's sexual promiscuity is widely believed to win respect from other men, while women who behave in similar ways are supposed to be regarded as contemptible.

Gender roles and sexual behaviour

The 'double standard', to the extent that it does exist, might be seen as advantageous and unproblematic for men. However, the explicit and implicit demands of the male gender role serve to restrict and constrain the choices of men as do the differing demands placed on women. Traditional masculinity, in at least some of its manifestations, places clear demands on a man to engage in indiscriminate predatory sexual behaviour, and other related activities such as drinking heavily, spending freely and boasting about sexual conquests. A man who fails to subscribe to the demands of a socially defined role thus thus runs the risk of becoming an object of mockery and contempt by other men. At an even more basic level, indiscriminate sexual behaviour places the individual at risk of sexually transmitted infections.

Even in societies that accept a range of definitions of 'appropriate' masculinities and have less rigid definitions of acceptable sex roles, expectations about the way men and women should behave tend to be most prescriptive and most gender-differentiated with reference to sexual behaviour (Blackwood 2000). Thus in western societies there has been a general expectancy that women should be relatively passive sexually. Investigating the impact of spinal cord injury on women's sexual functioning, Harrison *et al.* (1995) cited a 1960s report which epitomized gender-based assumptions about sexual behaviour, arguing that '. . . women's recovery is less problematic because they play a passive role in sexual intercourse . . .' (p. 687). Such stereotypes, it was argued, perpetuated a myth that spinal cord injury was less traumatic for women and inhibited research in the field.

Correspondingly there is a belief that men should initiate sexual activity, determine the form of such activity, and (usually after male orgasm) decide when a given sexual episode should cease. Such notions extend to encompass all sex-related behaviour, from the earliest stages of courtship. It is expected that the man will be the person who initiates a romantic relationship, the man who will initiate physical intimacy, and so forth. A man who lacks the confidence to take such a lead role runs the risk not only of failing to develop any intimate relationship, but also of perceiving himself, and being perceived by others, as a failure as a man. Correspondingly, men who have internalized such roles and values may find themselves unable to cope in a society where social norms for women have changed. Traditional gender roles therefore serve to restrict and impair the sexuality of men as well as of women.

Again, it should be noted that cultural expectations about men's greater sexual needs or drives are not necessarily reflected in individual attitudes. The idea that it is somehow 'natural' for men, and not women, to want sex with many partners is undermined by research on relationship infidelity (Treas and Giesen 2000) that demonstrates that sexual infidelity is accounted for by permissive sexual values, opportunities for sexual activity, and low levels of relationship satisfaction. Once these variables are taken into account, there are no gender differences. Similarly, a national survey of US men and women demonstrated that high-risk sexual behaviour such as sex with multiple sexual partners, unprotected sexual activity and casual sex could be explained by social and cultural factors rather than by gender (Cubbins and Tanfer 2000). If men are more likely than women to behave promiscuously, it is because of differences in opportunity, not in sexual interest.

Several surveys (for example Oliver and Hyde 1993; Schmidt *et al.* 1998; Milhausen and Herold 1999) find that men and women report equal levels of sexual desire and pleasure. Further, there is little evidence that women find sexual promiscuity attractive in a man; Milhausen and Herold (1999), in a survey of US college students, found that women positively rejected men who had had multiple sexual partners, a finding which further undermines the notion of a 'double standard' in contemporary society.

Gender roles, sexual behaviour and health

Not only is the notion of a 'real man' as heterosexually active and promiscuous problematic for those men who are unable or unwilling to conform to expectations, but also problems arise for those men who do adopt such a role. Acting in accordance with the view that masculinity is defined, in part, by the number of one's sexual partners increases the risk of exposure to sexually transmitted infections. The most commonly occurring sexually transmitted infections vary somewhat between countries, but in Australia they are chlamydia, genital herpes and genital warts (Donovan *et al.* 1998).

Most social research on sexually transmitted infection, however, has concentrated on HIV/AIDS; despite increasingly effective treatments in western countries, HIV/AIDS still has a significant death rate and is a major cause of death worldwide (Heymann 1995). The 'safe sex' practices advocated for prevention of the transmission of HIV/AIDS, however, are also effective in preventing the transmission of less dramatic infections. These include the avoidance of multiple sexual partners and avoidance of sexual activities (such as anal sex) that involve a high probability of tissue damage; while the consistent use of condoms should prevent these behaviours from spreading infection, it is obvious that condoms do occasionally fail.

Although knowledge about the use of condoms to prevent infection is widespread, social psychologists have established that men's intentions to use condoms, and their motivations to put those intentions into action, tend – unsurprisingly – to be reduced by a combination of alcohol use and sexual arousal (MacDonald *et al.* 2000). In fact, social psychological models of behaviour that assume that actions result from an individual's weighting of cognitive variables to arrive at a decision and then acting in accordance with that decision have been shown to be singularly inappropriate in explaining sex-related behaviour.

For example, a meta-analysis of the extent to which variables hypothesized by the Theory of Reasoned Action and its later development, the Theory of Planned Behaviour, predicted intended and actual use of condoms showed that the relationships are generally moderate (Albarracin *et al.* 2001). Individual attitudes alone do not predict condom use, and the

data strongly indicate a need to investigate the interpersonal and environmental factors that affect decision-making in sexual situations in order to
understand why people do, or do not, negotiate safe sexual activity.

Among young unmarried people, males are more reluctant than females
to suggest the use of condoms (for example Troth and Peterson 2000). This
is partly explained by beliefs that men's sexual pleasure is reduced by the
use of condoms, and also by the tendency among heterosexuals to view
condoms as primarily for contraception rather than infection control (the
implicit assumption of the alternative, that one of the partners has a sexually
transmissible infection, is stigmatizing and not compatible with cultural
scripts concerning romance and sex). Contraception is widely regarded,
at least by men, as the sole concern of women. Hooke *et al.* (2000), for
example, showed that teenage boys viewed contraception as a female responsibility, even though girls were likely to see it as a joint responsibility.
This asymmetry, and the greater social power which men's attitudes have
than women's, is reflected in a general cultural view that contraception is
an issue that concerns only women, as illustrated by the Canadian Contraception Study (Fisher *et al.* 1999), a survey of women only.

Again, this gender asymmetry in responsibility does not unproblematically
benefit men by burdening women; rather, it increases the risk that men will
put themselves at risk of infection. Newman and Zimmerman (2000),
for example, examined patterns of sexual behaviour among young urban
African Americans, and found that males were more likely than females to
meet criteria for high-risk sexual activity, using condoms inconsistently as
well as having multiple partners and having sex with strangers.

Homosexual men, who have the highest rates of HIV infection, are generally better than heterosexual men at practising safe sex, especially within
permanent relationships, if they know themselves or their partners to
be infected (for example Cusick and Rhodes 2000). But there are times
when sexual pleasure, intimacy and the expression of love are seen as more
important than the prevention of HIV transmission, and even couples of
mixed HIV status do on occasion engage in unsafe activity despite the risks
(Carballo-Dieguez *et al.* 1997; Cusick and Rhodes 2000).

Among homosexual men who are not in relationships, unsafe sexual
activity is even more of a health problem. Increasingly effective treatments
for HIV are paradoxically leading to higher rates of risky behaviour among
such groups (for example Dodds *et al.* 2000). This is a matter for concern,
as treatment continues to be expensive and remains unavailable in many
countries; it is not always entirely effective, and has unpleasant side-effects;
further, there are realistic concerns that resistant strains of HIV may develop (Grulich 2000).

Gay men's involvement in high-risk sexual activities, such as unprotected
penetrative sex with multiple, unknown partners, is somewhat difficult to
explain. Sexual behaviour is strongly influenced by its physical and social
setting, and settings such as bath-houses, public lavatories and parks appear

to support unsafe behaviour and promote the use of alcohol and other drugs which allow men to disengage from a sense of responsibility for their actions (Flowers *et al.* 2000; Williams *et al.* 2000). While these behaviours are dangerous and self-destructive, they are supported by a subculture that places value on these activities and minimizes the risks, to the extent that men who engage in these activities are more concerned about the risk of assault or arrest than they are about the risk of infection (Flowers *et al.* 1999).

It is not only with respect to the obvious problems of sexually transmitted infection, however, that adherence to stereotypes of masculinity produces problems relating to men's sexuality. In their groundbreaking study of the treatment of sexual dysfunctions, Masters and Johnson (1970) highlighted the role of 'performance anxiety' as a factor in producing and maintaining psychosexual problems. To the extent that men are expected, or perceive themselves as expected, to take the lead in sexual activity, there is a significant likelihood that they will experience doubts as to their ability and therefore become anxious. Since anxiety and sexual arousal are difficult to maintain simultaneously, anxiety is likely to interfere with sexual functioning, thereby producing greater anxiety on subsequent occasions, with greater risk of failure, reduced confidence and a vicious cycle of sexual inadequacy. Such an issue is of particular importance given strong cultural assumptions that 'proper' sexual activity must be initiated by a man and involve the insertion of the penis into a female partner's bodily orifice. Unless the penis is erect, insertion will be impossible, and if anxiety prevents erection, the man is likely to see himself as sexually incapable.

An alternative value system, one that did not assume that the man must be the dominant and directing partner in sexual activity and adopted a broader definition of sexual activity, would eliminate these sources of anxiety. Such a perspective would mean that any lack of satisfaction with the sexual encounter would be less likely to be seen as the male partner's fault, but as a problem of communication or compatibility between both partners. Such observations were exploited with great success by Masters and Johnson in their treatment programmes, in which couples were forbidden to attempt penile insertion during the early stages of treatment, thereby removing a major source of performance anxiety. Such an approach, however, fails to address the root of psychosexual problems in a society in which sexual activity is associated with marked gender imbalances and entangled with issues of power and status.

Living the gender role: sexual violence

As with other crimes of violence, the overwhelming majority of sexual offences are committed by men. Women are the victims in the majority of cases (Victoria Police 1997). But the fact that men are generally the perpetrators of such offences should not be interpreted as meaning that sexual violence is a problem only for women, or indeed only for those people – male and female – who are victims of these crimes. At the most simplistic level, men who are guilty of sexually violent crimes may experience arrest, trial, conviction and in some cases imprisonment, with all the social stigma and exposure to unsafe environments that this entails (Weisbuch 1991). At another level, the existence of a sexually violent society means that men who internalize the view that it is their role to protect women from assault are likely to experience anxiety, guilt and a sense of failure if a woman they know is sexually assaulted. At a more complex level, sexual assault can be viewed as a logical extension of assumptions that 'natural' sexual relationships between men and women should be adversarial and coercive; these assumptions, epitomized by rape, serve to alienate men and women from each other. Perhaps the most obvious of these are the assumptions that men are unable to control their sexuality, and that sex – for men – is equated with power. Sexual offending is predominantly an act of aggression and dominance rather than one of responding to sexual drive; Groth et al. (1977) in a study of rapists and victims concluded that in no case was sex the primary motivation, with power and anger predominating as motives. If men equate masculinity with a strong and uncontrollable sex drive, then they will see their sexuality as beyond their control (for it to be controllable would be tantamount to being unmasculine); and if they also equate masculinity with superiority over women, they will believe that they have some right to assert their physical strength or social power in order to engage in sex (Hill and Fischer 2001).

It is well established that both men and women view women as responsible for controlling access to sexual activity (Sorenson and White 1992). It is also well established that men perceive women's behaviour to imply sexual invitation much more than do the women themselves (for example Bostwick and DeLucia 1992; DeSouza et al. 1992). Men frequently misinterpret friendly or neutral behaviour on the part of women as signalling sexual interest. This may explain why men are more likely than women to believe that women are responsible for becoming the victims of criminal sexual assault (Johnson et al. 2000; Smith and Welchans 2000). If men, as it seems, are socialized to believe that activities such as smiling, wearing fashionable clothes, talking to men, drinking alcohol or going out at night are signals that women are interested in having sex, while women see them as neutral (Holcomb et al. 1991; Davis and Lee 1996), it is unsurprising that misunderstandings arise between men and women. And if men believe they have some entitlement to sexual activity if their expectations have been raised, as it appears they do, then these social myths and attitudes promote – indeed normalize – the occurrence of sexual assault (Hill and Fischer 2001).

Men are more likely than women to endorse 'rape myths', beliefs that women are responsible for being raped, that women want to be raped, and that women frequently make false accusations of rape (for example Feltey *et al.* 1991; Davis and Lee 1996). Men are also more likely to believe that there are circumstances in which it is acceptable for a male to force a female to have sex with him (Queensland Domestic Violence Resource Centre 1992; Johnson *et al.* 2000). Davis and Lee (1996) demonstrated that these gender differences in attitudes were found among schoolchildren as young as 14 years of age, suggesting that they arise from cultural images rather than from personal experience. This evidence supports a view of a culture that commodifies sex as something that women have and men want, and that sees sexual relationships as essentially adversarial and sexual violence as normal. Sexual assault is sanctioned by social myths and attitudes which obscure its violent and criminal nature (Leidig 1992) and create a culture in which assault is seen as an extension of normal male–female interaction (Bridges 1991).

Acquaintance sexual assault appears to be the most common form of sexual assault. Between 44 and 78 per cent of American college women report having had sexual contact with a date or acquaintance against their will (for example Miller and Marshall 1987; Muehlenhard and Linton 1987; Koss 1993) while between 7 and 25 per cent of college males report having forced sexual intercourse on a woman (Koss and Oros 1982; Rapaport and Burkhart 1984; Miller and Marshall 1987; Muehlenhard and Linton 1987). Muehlenhard and Linton (1987) found that 57 per cent of college men had engaged in sexually assaultive behaviour, while 17 per cent had attempted to engage in sexual behaviour against their partner's wishes on their most recent date.

People with traditional gender-role orientations have been shown to be more accepting of physical sexual coercion (Koss and Oros 1982; Garrett-Gooding and Senter 1987). A traditional and restrictive view of what constitutes appropriate conduct for women is associated with high acceptance of rape myths (for example Shotland and Goodstein 1983; Muehlenhard *et al.* 1985). Males score significantly higher than females on measures of traditional attitudes toward women's roles (Galambos *et al.* 1985) and, interestingly, most research finds that convicted rapists score no differently from other men (for example Harmon *et al.* 1991; Epps *et al.* 1993). Males also score significantly higher than females on tolerance of sexual harassment, coercion and assault, belief that heterosexual relationships are basically adversarial, and acceptance of sexual assault myths (for example Feltey *et al.* 1991). Thus, men are more likely to view incidents of sexual assault as justifiable and to believe that women are themselves to blame if they are assaulted.

The picture that emerges is one in which traditional gender roles not only create the conditions that make sexual assaults more likely, but also create a confusion between sex and power that constitutes a problem in general with respect to sexual functioning. The result is a distortion of sexuality that impacts negatively on both men and women. For some this distortion and confusion is resolved by formalizing of the parallel, as in bondage, discipline and sadomasochism (BDSM) or dominance/submission (D/S) scenes. For others the confusion is less obvious but none the less problematic, and may manifest itself in such behaviour patterns as domestic rape, familial incest, sexual abuse of children and so on, where positions in which one person has power over another become ones in which sexual exploitation occurs. While these arguments are usually raised in order to illustrate the damage that a patriarchal society does to women (for example Brownmiller 1975), it is also the case that misunderstandings between the genders, in the context of male power and assumptions about men's sexual needs, have the potential to cause emotional harm to men.

Alternative sexual preferences

One of the more prevailing and tenacious myths regarding male sexuality is that 'normal' men are exclusively heterosexual, with a minority of men either being homosexual or possibly bisexual. Commonly such identities are seen as essential and fundamental, an intrinsic, enduring and deep-seated characteristic of any given individual. A corollary of this perspective is that homosexual and bisexual men are deviant, to be excluded from the society of other men and indeed, in a very real sense, from society at large.

It is interesting that such a myth has proved resistant to challenge in spite of both conceptual problems and empirical challenges. At a conceptual level it becomes apparent that terms such as 'homosexual' are problematic; in particular it may be necessary to distinguish such things as homosexual behaviour, homosexual identity, homosexual attraction and homosexual lifestyle, especially as these will not necessarily all be apparent within a single individual. For example, a man may be sexually aroused by other men but refrain from sexual contact with them; such a man would exhibit no homosexual behaviour, but might reasonably claim a homosexual identity in the same way that another celibate man might claim to be heterosexual.

Empirically, too, such a categorization turns out to be problematic. Even in the pioneering surveys of the Kinsey Institute (Kinsey et al. 1948) it was acknowledged that there was a need to recognize degrees of homosexuality. Cross-cultural research indicates a considerable variation between societies in the amount of homosexual behaviour which takes place, sometimes in an institutionalized form, highlighting the fact that whether or not an individual exhibits homosexual behaviour may relate as much to the environmental context as to any supposed essential characteristic, an observation reflected by the increased likelihood of homosexual behaviour in prisons, where a sustained period without heterosexual contact is enforced.

Yet despite these observations, the notion that individuals can conveniently and intrinsically be classified as homosexual, bisexual or heterosexual continues to hold sway. A significant consequence of this is that a man who expresses any interest in same-sex sexual activity is likely to feel that this more than anything determines his own sense of identity, a process intensified by the hostility expressed by the wider community towards homosexual behaviour. Moreover this aspect of the man's identity will often be viewed as dominant – the man is, before he anything else, homosexual.

Inevitably, stepping outside the barriers of convention in this way brings with it all the stresses and difficulties of being part of a group regarded as deviant by the broader community, particularly for members of ethnic groups that stigmatize homosexuality to a very great extent (Kanuaha 2000). Such hostility can be encountered at an early age; awareness of same-sex attraction may occur between ages of 8 and 11, followed by first same-sex sexual behaviours between ages of 12 and 15 and disclosure to family members at around 18 to 19 (Savin-Williams and Diamond 2000). Hostility from others is frequent, with gay youths reporting being physically and verbally abused and robbed by family members, peers and faculty staff in colleges (Savin-Williams 1994). Surveys have reported the risk of suicidal ideation and suicide attempts among gays and lesbians to be as much as six times that of the general population (Remafedi et al. 1998; Fergusson et al. 1999), even when a range of confounding factors are controlled for by the use of twin studies (Herrell et al. 1999).

Unsurprisingly in a population where high levels of stress lead to increased prevalence of suicidality, the use of other unhealthy coping strategies is also apparent. Research has shown high rates of drug and alcohol use among those identifying as homosexual. Skinner (1994) found that two-thirds of a sample of 18- to 25-year-old gay men smoked cigarettes, all drank alcohol, and there were high rates of illicit drug use. These included not only recreational drugs such as marijuana but also misuse of medicinal drugs (for example tranquillizers, analgesics and psychotherapeutics). In addition to these, the use of inhalants or 'poppers' (amyl and butyl nitrite) is widespread, with the same study reporting 61 per cent of gay men using these at some point. High levels of drug use, and associated health problems, not only may be understood in terms of coping with societal rejection, but also may be explained by the fact that individuals who are excluded from mainstream society will feel less constrained by the rules, laws and values of that society.

At the same time, men who are attracted to other men will nevertheless often subscribe to other traditional notions of masculinity and indeed may emphasize these to a marked degree – 'if you're going to go for a man, go for a *real* man'. The man seeking others who are attracted to men may thus become hypermasculine – manifest not only in spending hours in the gym (and possibly becoming involved in such activities as illicit steroid use) building up a muscular body, but also in extensive sexual promiscuity, as discussed earlier with reference to the risks of sexually transmitted infections. Of course, no matter how much a gay man subscribes to a masculine image, he will continue to be unacceptable to 'normal' society; the centrality of sexuality in western society means that this, before anything else, will be seen as determining his identity and thereby his acceptability.

It is not only those with same-sex attractions who are seen as falling outside the norms and failing to live up to a 'masculine' ideal. Any man who steps outside the boundaries of male sexual conventions is likely to feel the need to hide this from his peers. This has the consequence not only of increasing the feeling of isolation of such men, but also of perpetuating the myth that most men conform to cultural norms of sexual behaviour. Any deviation from this is likely to be met with ridicule or indeed physical violence, with the result that men's freedom of choice in sexual expression, and their opportunities for peer comparison, are inevitably curtailed.

Alternatives to traditional perspectives

There is no doubt that it is possible to bring about changes in societal attitudes towards sexual behaviour. Indeed, such changes are readily apparent (for example Schmidt *et al.* 1998). In the light of such a possibility, it is worth considering what changes in societal views of male sexuality might prove beneficial, especially in terms of men's health. Men need to recognize the ways in which they are disadvantaged by traditional expectations about male sexual behaviour. They also need to understand the potential benefits for themselves, as well as for their relationships with women and for the promotion of a more equitable and less violent society, in challenging these.

Conclusion

This chapter argues that if men are to lead lives in which they are able to find, and share, sexual satisfaction without risk to psychological or physical well-being, they will need to re-evaluate traditional roles and practices, reject the conflation of sex and power and become more open and accepting of patterns of sexual behaviour which do not conform to current restrictive norms. Such changes would require a fundamental reorientation of cultural values and attitudes. The blame for dysfunctional sexual behaviours cannot be ascribed to individual men, but at the same time it is only through individual change that societies change.

Summary

- Gender differentiation in social behaviour is perhaps stronger for those behaviours related to sexual activity than for any other aspect of human social behaviour.

♦ Cultural stereotypes dictate that a 'real' man is motivated by a strong, uncontrollable biological sexual drive, seeks a wide range of sexual activities with as wide a range of female partners as possible, and takes a predatory and aggressive approach to sexual relationships. Although these stereotypes are not supported by the evidence on men's actual behaviour, they continue to restrict men's choices and expectations.

♦ Evidence from a range of countries and time periods indicates that gender differences in sexual attitudes and behaviour are more affected by culture and material conditions than they are by biological differences between men and women.

♦ While men vary in the extent to which they internalize cultural stereotypes about sexual behaviour, it appears that men are more likely than women to engage in high-risk sexual activity, placing them at risk of sexually transmitted infections.

♦ Cultural expectations about sexual behaviour also promote an expectation that only particular types of sexual activity are 'real' or 'normal' sex, placing pressure on men whose interests or preferences may be different.

♦ Assumptions that sexual relationships between men and women should be adversarial and aggressive, and that sex is a way in which men express power over women, produce a culture in which the lines between 'normal' sexual relationships and male aggression are ill-defined. Thus, sexual violence is normalized and sex is problematized for both men and women.

♦ Despite some change in social expectations, heterosexuality continues to be positioned as 'normal' and homosexuality, particularly among men, is strongly stigmatized, leading to a range of health risks and emotional difficulties for men who identify as homosexual.

♦ The evidence suggests that strong gender differentiation in sexual attitudes and behaviours is inimical to men's health and to their ability to maintain healthy sexual relationships, and that less prescriptive cultural attitudes to sexuality would benefit the health of all men.

Additional reading

Cubbins, L.A. and Tanfer, K. (2000) The influence of gender on sex: a study of men's and women's self-reported high-risk sex behavior, *Archives of Sexual Behavior*, 29: 229–57.
Oliver, M.B. and Hyde, J.S. (1993) Gender differences in sexuality: a meta-analysis, *Psychological Bulletin*, 114: 29–51.
Sorenson, S.B. and White, J.W. (1992) A sociocultural view of sexual assault: from discrepancy to diversity, *Journal of Social Issues*, 48: 187–95.

CHAPTER 6

Men and their bodies

It is not difficult to make the case that, compared to women, men have a much easier time when it comes to body image. Patriarchal societies position men as important and valuable in their own right, but value women in terms of their relationships with, and value to, men (Millett 1970). Women are implicitly positioned as 'other', as objects to be looked at rather than as individuals whose subjectivity is of equal value to that of men (Wooley 1994). Thus, one might assume that appearance-related issues will be particularly concerning for women but unproblematic for men. This chapter challenges this assumption, illustrating that men's relationships with their bodies are far from simple and far from unproblematic.

Women, to a much greater degree than men, are bombarded with an assortment of idealized images of what their bodies should look like. Many, if not most, women's magazines will contain pictures of women whose appearance (implicitly or explicitly) the readers are expected to aspire to. Similar images abound in TV programmes, films, advertising and other media (Rothblum 1994). By contrast, men's magazines, advertising directed at men, and other media designed for men are likely to show, not idealized men's bodies, but yet more of the idealized woman. The message is, apparently, simple: men look, and women are looked at. One might expect, therefore, that body image would be less of an issue for men, and that by and large men might not show the same kinds of concerns about their bodies as women do.

The evidence, however, suggests a more complex relationship between men, their bodies, and sociocultural expectations. Body image issues cannot be ignored when considering the male population. This chapter addresses a number of questions. What concerns do men have about their body image? To what extent do men see themselves as falling short of some particular ideal, and if they do so, how (if at all) does this impact upon their physical and emotional health? What factors produce body image concerns in men, and to what extent do male body image concerns parallel, and differ from, female body image concerns? Perhaps most importantly, how might such concerns can be addressed and alleviated?

Body image

While there is substantial evidence that men are less concerned about their body image than are women, this is not to say that such concerns do not exist for men. Even at an early age boys, like girls, frequently perceive their bodies as deviating from an internalized ideal. Even among children as young as 6, several large surveys of US children (Thompson *et al*. 1997; Gardner *et al*. 1999) found that both boys and girls evaluated themselves as being bigger than their ideal, although the discrepancy was considerably greater for the female children. But for all children, even at such an early age, there was a perception that they were already heavier than they wanted to be. By contrast, Tiggemann and Wilson-Barrett (1998) found no significant difference between perceived and ideal self among Australian boys aged 7 to 12, although such a discrepancy was found for girls. This difference in results may reflect a genuine cultural difference between US and Australian children, or may simply reflect the fact that the Australian samples were relatively small and thus that the effects failed to reach statistical significance.

Although the Australian survey is quite small, it supports other research showing cultural differences in the extent of concerns about body size. It has been well established, for example, that African American women aspire to somewhat larger body sizes than White American women, and that African American men prefer women's body sizes which are somewhat larger than the shapes preferred by White American men (Harris *et al*. 1991). Interestingly, Thompson *et al*. (1997) found that African American boys, relative to White American boys, specified a heavier ideal for themselves, as well as identifying themselves as heavier than the white children.

Among adults, the research again demonstrates that women place more importance than men on physical appearance (Smith *et al*. 1999) and that cultural constructions of the relationship between women, men and their bodies are internalized by both genders. As with children, the majority of research with adults has been with female rather than male participants, with few studies including males and none focusing entirely on men. This lack of interest in men's body image reflects an uncritical acceptance by mainstream psychology of hegemonic models of masculinity, and of cultural assumptions about men and their emotional concerns.

Because men are positioned as unconcerned about their appearance, it is assumed that men will not have body image problems. Yet this assumption conflicts both with the evidence reviewed below, and with other aspects of hegemonic masculinity. Culturally favoured models of maleness include an injunction to conform to a mesomorphic body type: athletic, muscular and with low body fat (Petersen 1998).

The evidence, although limited, does suggest that men, like women, demonstrate a degree of discrepancy between their perceptions of themselves as they are and their perceptions of how they would ideally like to be. Moreover, in some groups at least the degree of body dissatisfaction among males appears to be higher than among females. However, there is an important differece. Where women overwhelmingly wish to be thinner (for example Lee 2001), men typically wish to be heavier. For example, Abell and Richards (1996) found significantly higher levels of body dissatisfaction among young men than among young women, and found that the men typically wanted to be heavier and larger. This of course contrasts with the results of the studies of children mentioned earlier, where both sexes expressed a wish to be thinner.

Such a shift in ideal body shape between childhood and adulthood should not be surprising. The social comparison literature suggests that people are likely to compare themselves with their peers, rather than with society as a whole (Wilcox 1997). Because prepubertal boys are biologically unlikely to develop significant muscularity, and young boys are likely to compare themselves with other boys of the same age, they are unlikely to perceive themselves as insufficiently muscular. If a prepubertal boy's peer group comments unfavourably on body shape, it is likely to be adiposity rather than lack of muscularity that is the main target of jibes. Thus for prepubertal children, male or female, the prevailing desire is likely to be for greater thinness.

Following puberty, however, the child may become more conscious of the variability among his peers. Boys who are slow to develop may compare themselves with other boys of the same chronological age who have already reached puberty and shown significant increases in muscularity and size, thus reaching the conclusion that their bodies are unsatisfactory because they are too small. Thus, one would predict that as male children passed through puberty, there would be for some a shift in body concerns from a wish to be thinner to a wish to be more muscular. There is a need for longitudinal research on male concerns about body image before, during and after puberty in order to determine whether, and if so when, such changes take place, and to explore the relationships between individual boys' body concerns and the extent of their exposure to, and internalization of, stereotyped images of attractive men as large and muscular.

This concern about muscularity and bulk is likely to begin before puberty. Children's exposure to media images means that boys are likely to become conscious of the social value placed on muscle bulk well before they and their peers enter puberty, but the extent to which this awareness has any personal meaning may be relatively low, until they begin to see changes in themselves or their peers.

Certainly studies of adult males indicate that the discrepancy between self-perception and ideal may be complex. While overweight individuals of either sex generally wish to be thinner, Raudenbush and Zellner (1997) found that nearly 42 per cent of healthy-weight men wished to be heavier (by contrast, nearly 88 per cent of healthy-weight women wished to be lighter). Another aspect of male body image which is clearly influenced by cultural expectations and concerns about inadequacy, that of penis size, has been the subject of remarkably little epidemiological research, although the evidence that the average man considers his own penis to be somewhat smaller than average (Lee 1996) indicates that men do tend to have concerns about this aspect of their anatomy. Men's body image concerns do appear to involve considerably more than fat and muscle, although these have received most of the research attention to date.

Smith *et al.* (1999), in a large survey of US adults' cardiovascular risk factors, demonstrated that, as expected, adult men and women were generally concerned to reduce fat. But the situation for males and females in the thinnest 25 per cent of the population was very different, both according to gender and according to race. White American women, even at the thinnest end of the population, still expressed a wish to weigh less. This is consistent with evidence from other developed countries (for example Lee 2001). Thin African American women, by contrast, showed hardly any discrepancy at all between their perceived and ideal weight. For both African American and White American men, however, the pattern was markedly different. Thinner White American men were just as dissatisfied as White women, but wanted to weigh more, not less. Although thinner African American men were less dissatisfied than thin White men, they were actually more dissatisfied than the thinnest African American women (the only group of women to show lower dissatisfaction than the corresponding men). Again, the men wanted to be bigger, rather than smaller. This evidence suggests that being underweight is particularly stigmatizing for African American men.

Such findings also suggest that men's relationships with their bodies are more complex than women's. For a woman, body fat is the single crucial issue, and it is difficult or impossible to be too thin. For a man, however, both fat and muscle are important, and it is possible to be too thin or too fat. Indeed, it is possible for a man to be simultaneously too thin *and* too fat, in the sense that he has both less muscle and more fat than he would ideally like. Interestingly this effect does not appear to be restricted to western cultures, with Davis and Katzman (1998) showing that Hong Kong Chinese men's level of weight dissatisfaction was greater than that of women, with the majority of the men wishing to be larger. Thus, men's body image concerns may be as great as, or greater than, those among women and may also be more complex. Women, it appears, are motivated to reduce body fat, while men are motivated both to reduce fat and to increase musculature. This suggests that a larger range of weight-change strategies, not all of them healthy, may be demonstrated by men.

Body dissatisfaction and men's health

The consistent finding that men's bodies are often not entirely to their satisfaction does not necessarily mean that this discrepancy between ideal and real causes them any significant distress. Certainly a considerable amount of evidence indicates that body dissatisfaction in women is associated with problems of various kinds (Rothblum 1994). The relative importance of physical appearance for men and women in patriarchal societies (Harris *et al.* 1991), however, might suggest that men could recognize a discrepancy between actual and ideal, without being significantly concerned about it.

Some evidence, however, exists that men, like women, find that body dissatisfaction impacts upon their well-being. Several independent research projects (Abell and Richards 1996; Davis and Katzman 1997; Henriques and Calhoun 1999) have shown that men and women show moderate, and approximately equal, correlations between body image and self-esteem. Interestingly, some researchers have reported a stronger relationship between body image and self-esteem for males than for females. Tiggemann and Wilson-Barrett (1998), in a study of Australian children, for example, found no relationship between body dissatisfaction and self-esteem for girls but a significant negative correlation for the boys. Davis and Katzman (1997), with Hong Kong Chinese students, and Abell and Richards (1996), with a US sample, found broadly similar and significant correlations between self-esteem and body dissatisfaction measures for men and women. Thus, men do appear to be affected emotionally by poor body image. This section explores the extent to which this may affect men's health. Again, there is a vast literature that addresses this question for women, and a relative dearth of research on men. The perception that men should not be concerned about body shape appears to be reflected in a relative neglect of the effects of body dissatisfaction on men's physical and emotional health.

Losing weight

Clinical eating disorders such as anorexia nervosa and bulimia nervosa have been exhaustively explored, but this has been largely within the female population, to the extent that males are simply ignored in a large proportion of this research. Certainly the evidence consistently indicates a substantially higher prevalence of eating disorders among women than men, with studies reporting a range of gender distributions but rarely more than 10 per cent of anorexic and 20 per cent of bulimic individuals being male (for example Hsu 1990).

Both anorexia nervosa and bulimia nervosa certainly do occur in males (Buckley *et al.* 1991; Carlat and Camargo 1991). Men who develop eating disorders tend to be involved in occupations such as modelling or dancing, or sporting activities such as diving or horse racing, which demand low body fat; bulimia in particular seems more common in homosexual than heterosexual men (Carlat and Camargo 1991). The gendered nature of the development of the conditions may be confused, however, by biases in diagnosis.

Hepworth and Griffin (1995) have argued that contemporary medical discourses concerning anorexia nervosa and other eating disorders are so strongly gendered that men are much less likely than women to receive a diagnosis of anorexia or bulimia, despite objectively identical behaviour. Men with disordered eating, they argue, are more likely to be labelled as depressives with associated changes in appetite than to receive a primary diagnosis of eating disorder. Further, the same cultural preconception is likely to influence presentation rates. With respect to bulimia in particular, it is possible for an individual to conceal the problem for years without others becoming aware of it. Since it is seen as a 'female' problem, bulimic men may be extremely reluctant to admit to the problem and to seek help. Finally, the differences in underlying rates may be supported by cultural expectations about the gendered nature of the conditions. Bulimic and anorexic behaviours are relatively common in the female population and are widely discussed in women's magazines; thus, young women may adopt them as a result of real or perceived peer modelling of these behaviours. This acceptance of disordered eating behaviours as reasonably common appears to be relatively absent in the cultural and social experiences of young men, who thus may have fewer cues to experiment with them and to discuss them with their peers. While any one of these may have only a slight effect on reported prevalence rates, taken together they suggest the possibility that the level of disordered eating in men, although still below that in women, may be higher than it might appear.

Problematic or disordered weight-related behaviour certainly does occur among men. A large study of US adolescents (Story et al. 1995) demonstrated the existence of substantial levels of problematic weight control behaviours in both males and females, with 2 to 3 per cent of males dieting always or more than ten times per year, 5 to 14 per cent deliberately vomiting after eating, and 12 to 21 per cent with a history of binge eating. Although, as expected, most of these problem behaviours were more common among females (depending on the problem, the relative rates ranged from only slightly more common to six times as common), this was against a backdrop of a quite different body mass distribution. The males were much less likely to be overweight, and more likely to be underweight, than the females. Since underweight males are more likely to wish to increase weight, it is unsurprising that the men were less likely to exhibit problem weight-loss behaviours. It is worth noting that comparisons of the prevalence rates of eating problems between males and females have often failed to control for possible underlying real differences in the degree of overweight and underweight in the two groups.

Although middle-aged and older men are more likely to be overweight or obese than women of the same age (National Heart Foundation of Australia 1983), the opposite pattern is found among young adults and adolescents. If young men are generally underweight and want to be physically larger, they are obviously less likely to be trying to lose weight than women of the same age. While the evidence is clear that men are less likely than women to engage in unhealthy weight loss behaviours, then, research does need to be interpreted with some caution.

Studies of adult males with eating disorders have indicated a number of similarities with eating disordered women. Olivardia *et al.* (1995), studying 25 men with eating disorders (anorexia nervosa, bulimia nervosa or a combination), noted distinct similarities to comparable females in terms of variables such as age of onset, comorbidities, body dissatisfaction and attitude towards the eating disorder. However, they also noted that the men were significantly less likely than the women to have sought treatment. A subsequent replication of their US study in Austria (Mangweth *et al.* 1997) found similar results.

It has been argued that, if eating disorders arise from ambiguities and tensions inherent in the traditional female gender role and in mainstream expectations of women, homosexual men, susceptible to pressures to conform to a stereotype of attractiveness which is pleasing to other men, may be more at risk than heterosexual men (Schneider *et al.* 1995). In both the US and Austrian studies mentioned above, the researchers noted a somewhat higher incidence of homosexual men in the eating-disordered group, although in neither case was this difference statistically significant, probably as a result of small sample sizes. French *et al.* (1996) found that male adolescents who identified as homosexual showed poorer body image and higher rates of frequent dieting, binge eating and purging than a comparison heterosexual group. Other research supports this; studies of US college students (Siever 1994) and of San Francisco adults (Schneider *et al.* 1995) have found that homosexual men and heterosexual women are most vulnerable to eating disorders and most dissatisfied with their bodies. However, comprehensive reviews (Heffernan 1994, 1996) have concluded that results in this area are mixed and that definite conclusions regarding the role of sexual orientation in eating-related concerns cannot be reached. Homosexual people, after all, still live in a largely heterosexual society and are exposed to the same socialization processes, the same media images, and the same gendered expectations as are heterosexual people.

The higher rate of disordered eating among gay men, however, has been argued to relate to a greater emphasis placed by men than by women on physical attractiveness in a partner (for example French *et al.* 1996). Thus, both heterosexual women and homosexual men may be at greater risk for disturbed eating patterns as they endeavour to conform to a societal demand that individuals who have, or want, male partners have a responsibility to change their appearance in order to meet their expectations.

To summarize, then, a number of observations may be made regarding the risk of disturbed eating among men. First, although the evidence consistently indicates that eating disorders are more common in women than men, their prevalence among men may still be substantial, particularly when account is taken of possible under-reporting and under-detection. Second, it appears that disordered eating in males, as in females, can be detected at a relatively early age, and is associated with a 'drive for thinness'. Finally, there are clear differences between men's and women's eating problems. For males identifying as homosexual there is evidence of an increased prevalence of disturbed eating patterns by comparison with those identifying as heterosexual, while for females the relationship between sexuality and eating problems is considerably less clear. By far the most striking difference between males and females is that for men, body image concerns revolve not only around fat but also around muscularity. Thus for some men, there may be an internalization of cultural conceptions that men should be large, strong and muscular (Petersen 1998), resulting in a drive not to lose, but to gain weight, a drive which itself can give rise to special problems for men.

Gaining weight

The cultural imperative that men should be large and strong frequently manifests itself as a wish to gain weight, and in particular to gain muscle bulk. The development of muscularity is a complex process, involving interactions between exercise, diet and physiology. Like distribution of body fat, muscularity is to some extent limited by genetic factors that are not susceptible to change. The notion that the human body is infinitely perfectible, and that willpower alone can produce a body of any shape, may be responsible for considerable levels of stress and disordered behaviour among both men and women (Brownell 1991). Neither exercise, nor diet, nor underlying physiology relates in any simple way to the growth of muscularity, and an insufficiency in any one can result in lack of development. Further, each of these factors is complex and multifaceted; not all forms of exercise, for example, result in increases in bulk, and muscular size and strength are by no means identical to each other.

Perhaps the most obvious group of men pursuing muscular development through such a strategy is that of bodybuilders. The idea of increasing a man's muscular development became popularized in the 1940s, in particular as a result of the principles developed by Charles Atlas, whose 'dynamic tension' approach to exercise (an extension of isometric principles exploiting the use of opposed muscle pairs) promised a generation of '98 pound weaklings' that without the use of weights they could begin to see results in just seven days.

It was not long, however, before individuals pursuing extremes of muscle growth began to look beyond exercise and diet to the third component, physiology, and to ways of enhancing this too. Thus in the 1950s and 1960s athletes in sports requiring muscle bulk started to take anabolic steroids in order to maximize the benefits of training. Although by the mid-1970s sporting bodies such as the International Olympic Committee had largely declared the use of such drugs illegal, nevertheless their use continued, dramatically highlighted in 1988 with the disqualification of Ben Jonson, the 100 metre gold medallist at the Seoul Olympics, after he tested positive for the anabolic steroid Stanazolol. Although he was by no means the first Olympic athlete to test positive for anabolic steroids, Jonson's was an extraordinarily high profile, not least because of the status accorded to that particular event. Subsequent debate, particularly in his native Canada, not infrequently raised the argument that such drug-taking was endemic in top-level sport, and that the censuring of an individual was hardly fair in a context in which, it was argued, one needed to take drugs to keep up with one's opponents who were also doing so.

The use of steroids is by no means restricted to elite sports competitors. The cultural value placed on male muscularity is so high that men who have no practical need to be large and strong are still highly motivated to achieve a particular body type, and the use of steroids is one way of achieving this goal. The use of steroids in the normal male population may be seen as analogous in some ways to the use of disordered eating behaviours among women; it is becoming increasingly apparent that the use of anabolic steroids and other drugs is not confined to the top levels of competitive sport.

With the widespread use of illicit drugs in sport and exercise have come concerns about potential health risks associated with their use. Dramatic individual cases have had a major impact on public perceptions of the use of drugs in sport (International Olympic Committee 1999). A number of concerns have been raised about possible side-effects of the use of anabolic steroids, including liver disorders, changes in lipid metabolism causing increased risk of cardiovascular disease, and (in men) prostatic enlargement and development of breast tissue (gynaecomastia). There has also been some suggestion of increased risk of psychological disturbance, especially aggressive behaviour. While the evidence does suggest that the extent of these risks has been overstated (Sharp and Collins 1998; Owens 1999) there is sufficient evidence to give rise to concern, and a good case can be made that it is prudent to avoid the unnecessary use of anabolic steroids. Despite this, evidence suggests that steroids are widely used both within and outside competitive sport.

In the areas of competitive sport in which steroid use has most obvious benefits, rates may be so high as to be almost endemic. Blouin and Goldfield (1995) for example report that 78 per cent of their sample of competitive bodybuilders reported using anabolic steroids, as did 20 per cent of their recreational bodybuilders. In a study of 16- to 19-year-old students in Sweden, Kindlundh et al. (1999) found that 2.7 per cent of males reported having used anabolic-androgenic steroids. By contrast, Drewnowski et al. (1995) found that non-sporting adolescent males had a low (0.6 per cent) rate of steroid use.

Other researchers have reported a variety of rates in different groups. Wroblewska (1997), in a review of published survey research, found rates ranging from 4 per cent of males in general to 75 per cent of competitive bodybuilders, and estimated that the US annual national spending on anabolic steroids for non-medical use would have been around $500 million in 1993. Even according to the most conservative estimates, therefore, it appears that a substantial number of males are, for no medical reason, ingesting substances which may carry significant health risks.

Evidence also exists to link such use to psychological and particularly to body-image issues, further strengthening the argument that the problem represents a parallel in males to anorexia and bulimia nervosa in females. Blouin and Goldfield (1995), for example, found psychological and body image variables to be significant predictors of steroid use in bodybuilders, and noted that their profile of body-related attitudes and psychological characteristics was similar to those of eating disorder patients. By contrast, Schwerin et al. (1996) found no differences in body dissatisfaction between steroid-using and non-steroid-using bodybuilders. This, however, may reflect nothing more than the use of steroids having the effect of reducing body dissatisfaction among those who chose to use them, while those who chose not to use them in the first place had made that decision because they were not dissatisfied with their bodies. The authors suggest that a concept such as 'drive for bulk', paralleling the notion of 'drive for thinness', may be of value in identifying those at risk for illicit anabolic steroid use.

Evidence such as this suggests that men are not unproblematically comfortable in their own bodies. For some men, the perceived need to aspire to a societal ideal of muscular masculinity may lead to unhealthy behaviours. The use of anabolic steroids to help achieve a culturally prescribed ideal carries potential health risks, risks which may be exacerbated by the fact that such use is illicit, with consequent lack of medical supervision, poor drug quality control (including the use of veterinary or out-of-date preparations) and possible interactions with other necessary medications. There are also risks of infection associated with the use of shared or otherwise non-sterile needles for intramuscular injections of steroids.

It was noted earlier, in the context of eating disorders in men, that some research supports the notion of higher prevalence of such disorders in men identifying as homosexual. If it is true that men who wish to attract other men will tend to be more concerned with their appearance, then one might expect that for a subset of gay men, at least, steroid use might be a particular problem. In particular, given the role of the gym as a social centre and meeting place in some gay communities the possibility for risk of steroid use may be raised further. Bolding et al. (1999), in a study of London gyms with a high attendance among gay men, found that between 2.7 per cent and 21.2 per cent of the respondents were current users of steroids, with 0.4 per cent to 17.5 per cent injecting. Interestingly, although none of the respondents reported using shared or non-sterile needles, those who injected were significantly more likely to report status-unknown unprotected anal intercourse. This might be explained by or a possible common underlying tendency towards risky behaviour resulting both in steroid use and risky sexual behaviour. Another possibility might be that for some men, the need to attract other men is so great that the risks are seen as worthwhile in order to achieve the outcomes. Whatever the explanation, it does suggest that at least some men – and gay men are again at increased risk – are placing themselves at risk in order to achieve what they consider to be a desirable body shape.

Overall, then, it appears that although for women, body image problems almost universally result in a drive for thinness and consequent risk of eating disorders, for men body image problems can result both in a drive for thinness among those men who see themselves as too fat, and a drive for bulk among men who see themselves as too thin. For men, therefore, body image problems can in one direction lead (though less frequently than for women) to eating disorders such as anorexia nervosa and bulimia nervosa; in the opposite direction (and more frequently than for women) to unhealthy weight gain practices such as steroid use.

Origin of body image problems in men

In considering body image problems in women, a number of researchers have pointed to the role of societal factors, and in particular the prevalence of role models emphasizing the importance of physical appearance in general, and slimness in particular (Rothblum 1994). While the asymmetries of a patriarchal society mean that exact parallels are unlikely to be entirely appropriate, it is still easy to see how societal role models can lead individual men to be dissatisfied with their bodies. Men are presented with the concept that a real man is large, hard and strong (Petersen 1998). Physical role models for men are not as prevalent as for women, but they are just as unhealthy and unrealistic: from the Charles Atlas physiques of the 1940s and 1950s, through the massive bodies of bodybuilder actors like Arnold Schwarzenegger to the hypermuscularity of present-day bodybuilders. With such images, men are presented with two clear messages as regards physical appearance; a low percentage body fat is seen as good, and a low muscle bulk is seen as bad.

Clearly, however, not all men develop such body image concerns, despite a society replete with such images, any more than all women do. If one is to understand why some men have problems, there is a need to understand the role of broader social expectations and the extent to which individual men do or do not internalize specific aspects of them.

There are many expectations that need to be met if a male is truly to be considered 'a man' in terms acceptable to traditional perceptions of masculinity. An apocryphal Japanese tale has a Samurai knight saying to his son,

'I would not have you a priest, of whom there are many, but a man, of whom there are few.' While a 'man' is expected to show many characteristics, some of which are mutually incompatible, high levels of muscularity are intrinsic to a number of the most salient characteristics. A man is expected to be a provider and a protector of his family. He is expected to compete with other men, not only in the formal senses of activities like sport and employment, but also informally for status within a social group. He is expected to be self-confident, at ease with himself. He is expected to be successful romantically, and in some social groups his status will be assessed at least in part by his success in attracting partners, whose social value is enhanced by their own level of attractiveness. Put most simply, a man should aim to be one who is envied by other men.

In reality, of course, these ideals are impossible for any individual to achieve and although there is an assumption that men are individually responsible for their success in life, it is obvious that social, economic and practical constraints will limit men's choices and opportunities. Given the conflicts between hegemonic cultural expectations of men and the social realities with which they must live, it is unsurprising if some men associate their failure to achieve these unrealistic social goals with perceived bodily inadequacies, with the implication that if only their bodies were closer to the ideal, their personal problems would somehow disappear.

An apparent weakness with arguments that link body image problems to social pressures and stereotypes is that both men and women who develop problematic behaviours continue these to a point which is clearly beyond social images of the ideal. To some extent such a criticism is justified, in that it illustrates the complexity of the underlying processes that link social images and individual behavioural choices. A number of hypotheses, not necessarily mutually exclusive, might identify characteristics which might lead individuals to continue their pursuit of a particular ideal beyond those valued by society.

First, there is evidence that men, particularly younger men, overestimate the male body size that women find attractive. Lynch and Zellner (1999) showed that college men tended to select hypermuscular body sizes as those which women would prefer; college women themselves preferred a male body size that was larger than average, but quite noticeably smaller than the shape that the men believed would be considered attractive. This effect was not found among middle-aged adults, supporting other evidence that body image disturbance and unhealthy behaviours tend to peak in the younger age groups. Misperception, both of the ideal, and of one's own body shape, may be one factor that leads to persistence with weight-changing behaviours far beyond an acceptable limit.

Second, for a number of men (and women), the 'going beyond' social ideals and aiming for an extreme body shape could in some sense be an act of defiance or resentment against social pressures to conform to a particular body type. There may be a level at which the individual deliberately goes beyond what is considered necessary to achieve an ideal, although as yet there has been no research to explore such a possibility.

Third, there may be some degree of behavioural momentum as a direct consequence of body changes. Factors that lead to the adoption of a behaviour and those that lead to its continuation are not necessarily identical, and Slade (1982) has suggested that a perception of weight loss may acquire reinforcing properties of its own, beyond those which are associated with reaching some ideal body shape. A related variable may be a feeling of control; individuals who feel that they have insufficient control over their lives may find the experience of being able to control their own body shape extremely reinforcing, such that the behaviour (dieting, exercising, purging or drug-taking) continues even after an ideal image has been achieved.

In understanding the development and maintenance of body image problems in men, therefore, we need (as with women) to recognize the complexity of the processes involved and the range of ways in which societal and individual factors may act together. The intense social pressure on men to 'be a man', to compete with other men, to be perceived as successful, means that men are impelled to find a field in which they can (even if only in relative terms) excel. For some men this will be in traditionally masculine areas such as sport, games, intellectual activities, or employment. Others however may regard their chances of success in these areas as relatively low, and efforts to succeed in terms of appearance may appear to be the most accessible strategy for achieving masculinity.

Where next

Traditionally, attempts to reduce or eliminate problems such as disordered eating or substance abuse have been directed at the individual level. Individuals diagnosed with eating disorders are pathologized and in consequence seen as in need of treatment. Increasingly there is an awareness within the psychological literature that women with clinical eating disorders are not qualitatively different from other women, but are more usefully seen as falling at one end of a continuum of concerns about weight, shape and eating that are present, to a greater or lesser degree, in the majority of women (Rodin et al. 1984). Even so, psychological models that accept the existence of social factors in disordered eating among women generally fail to engage in any serious analysis of these factors. When one turns to men with body image problems, the psychological literature is almost entirely silent at all levels from the individual to the sociocultural.

However, seen from a broader perspective, it is possible to recognize that these behaviours serve specific functions for the individual in terms of meeting the internalized demands of a gender role. Eliminating the problem behaviour in this context carries the risk that at best the individual will simply seek out another area of life in which to acquire status. For many individuals, attempts to succeed through manipulation of body size of shape will have been resorted to precisely because other potential areas of achievement have proved difficult. It may be recalled that this need to find a strategy for embodying a gender role, under circumstances in which positive strategies are unavailable, is the same explanation proposed by Messerschmidt (1993) to explain men's adoption of violence and criminal activity. Interventions which 'fix' unhealthy body-shape-related behaviours and attitudes, thus, may in fact have the consequence of causing even more harmful and antisocial behavioural choices.

Conclusion

This chapter demonstrates that men's relationships with their bodies are at least as complex as are those of women. Gendered expectations that men should be large and muscular affect the self-esteem of all men, and some groups (men who are physically small; homosexual men; men whose ability to enact gender roles in other ways are limited) experience severe distress and dysfunctional behaviour as a result. We argue for a broader recognition of the insidious effects that gender role expectations may have in this as in other areas of life, and for a more fundamental challenging of these role expectations, such that the individual can learn to reject these and instead to accept himself on his own terms.

Summary

- Men are less likely than women to experience problems related to body image, weight and appearance, but the evidence shows that men are by no means immune to the effects of gender stereotypes of appropriate appearance.
- In general men's body image is less negative than that of women, but there are particular issues for men who are below normal weight. While among women, body image issues revolve almost entirely around body fat, the issues for men are more complex, encompassing expectations that men should have both low levels of body fat and high levels of lean muscle mass.
- Among men, the relationship between low body image and low self-esteem is moderate, and is roughly equivalent to that found among women.
- Clinical eating disorders such as anorexia nervosa and bulimia nervosa are relatively uncommon among men, with prevalence rates around 10 per cent of that of women, but they do occur, particularly among men whose occupations or recreational interests revolve around a particular body type.

♦ Because men, unlike most women, are strongly motivated to increase muscle mass, men are much more likely than women to use anabolic steroids and related pharmaceuticals for non-medical reasons. While the medical effects of the misuse of these drugs are not clear, their use in this way illustrates a widespread discontent among men with normal, healthy body shape, that is analogous to dieting concerns among women.
♦ There is evidence that homosexual men are more likely than heterosexual men to experience poor body image, to engage in unhealthy eating behaviours, and to abuse steroids. It appears that homosexual men and heterosexual women are both strongly motivated to achieve a body type which will attract men, and that this motivation may be associated with unhealthy behaviour.
♦ Hegemonic masculinity specifies that a man should be large, strong and physically capable, with low body fat and large well-defined muscles. Even though most men in contemporary society have little practical need to be large and strong, this cultural stereotype promotes unhealthy behaviours in a substantial minority of men who are unable to conform to, or to resist, masculine gender role stereotypes without engaging in unhealthy behaviour.
♦ There is a need for greater awareness of the role of masculine gender role stereotypes in unhealthy weight-related behaviours among men.

Additional reading

Buckley, P., Freyne, A. and Walsh, N. (1991) Anorexia nervosa in males, *Irish Journal of Psychological Medicine*, 8: 15–18.
Petersen, A. (1998) *Unmasking the Masculine: 'Men' and 'Identity' in a Sceptical Age*. London: Sage, esp. ch. 3, Male bodies that matter.
Wroblewska, A.M. (1997) Androgenic-anabolic steroids and body dysmorphia in young men, *Journal of Psychosomatic Research*, 42: 225–34.

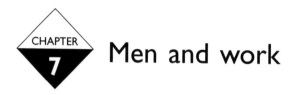

Men and work

In western capitalist societies, men are defined by 'what they do' – their paid occupation in the public sphere – rather than by who they are. A central tenet of hegemonic masculinity is the assumption that a 'real' man will have a full-time, permanent job – probably involving making something – which supports his family financially (Price *et al.* 1998). He will see his career as the most important aspect of his life, and will always be prepared to sacrifice family activities for work and for career advancement. As Coltrane (1989: 488) expressed it, the 'essential nature of men is taken to be that of provider' both by men themselves and by society more generally. Men who are unemployed or underemployed, who live in role-reversed or in same-sex relationships, or who otherwise do not conform to the stereotype of the man providing for wife and children, are stigmatized (for example Grbich 1992). This social stereotype has failed to keep up with the changed realities of work and family life, and many men are likely to experience stress and stress-related illness as a result of having to deal with conflict between social expectations and the reality of their personal and family lives.

Radical feminists have argued that capitalism and patriarchy are inimical to the best interests of women: that the dominant cultural discourses of patriarchal societies position men and women as essentially different, and that social institutions – including law, government, employment and childcare systems – militate against women's freedom to make optimal life choices (Riger 1992). These arguments can be extended to the position of men. Those men whose choices or life circumstances mean that they do not participate in the benefits of patriarchy are stigmatized, while those who do conform to social expectations are also unable to make genuinely unconstrained choices about their lives. This chapter explores issues surrounding work, both formal paid work and unpaid domestic labour, for men. It demonstrates that men's lives and choices are influenced by social and economic forces which are inimical to their health and to their intimate relationships.

Paid work

The psychological literature has not problematized men and paid work in the way that it has women and paid work. There is no literature which parallels the well-articulated theories and extensive research on multiple roles in women's lives (for example Baruch and Barnett 1986; Repetti *et al.* 1989). Research on the physical and emotional effects of paid work among women has focused on the difficulties faced by women who combine paid work, domestic labour, care of children and caregiving for frail or elderly family members (for example Doress-Worters 1994; Lundberg 1996). By contrast, psychological research concerned with men and paid employment has lacked a specifically gendered focus. With very few exceptions (for example Milkie and Peltola 1999), it has not to any useful extent examined the extent to which men's social roles might support or conflict with each other. In fact, researchers seem to accept uncritically the notion that men have only one role that matters – that of paid worker – and that any other roles are essentially optional and secondary, and can and should be abandoned at any time if the work role requires this.

Men's role conflicts between paid work and family responsibilities are seen as freely chosen and thus not as legitimate social problems. Again there is an asymmetry between the expectations placed on men and women: women's multiple roles are positioned as both problematic and unavoidable (Perry-Jenkins 1993); men are assumed to be able to drop all non-career roles at any time they choose.

Thus, psychological research has little to say on a range of work-related issues that confront men and their partners in contemporary society. These include role conflicts, but must also include men's reactions to systemic changes in the job market. These changes have led to increased levels of unemployment, underemployment, and loss of employment security among men (for example Australian Bureau of Statistics 1995), which undermine their ability to embody the cultural imperative that a man has a paid job. They also include men's individual efforts to cope with the inherent conflicts between a traditionally patriarchal society and the increased value placed on feminist and egalitarian worldviews. To what extent do men who consider themselves feminist or egalitarian in outlook experience guilt or conflict over continuing social inequity in both paid and unpaid work? What are men's preferences for and experiences of childcare and unpaid domestic labour in the context of their working lives?

More generally, psychology has ignored the conflicts experienced by men who have, to varying extents, internalized contradictory understandings of masculinity. The extent to which men in contemporary society struggle to reconcile traditional notions of masculinity as entailing difference from, and essential superiority to, women, with contemporary ideals of men as supportive, flexible and egalitarian, has been explored to some extent within sociology and cultural studies (for example Pleck 1977), but psychology has almost entirely ignored this conflict.

There is ample evidence that the 'traditional' division of labour, with men in full-time paid careers and women's main or only responsibilities for unpaid work inside the home, having to fit any paid work around what is seen as their 'primary' job, benefits men economically (Apter 1993). Employed men are paid more than employed women, both in absolute terms and on an hour-by-hour basis, and are more likely to be in jobs which provide paid overtime, training opportunities, commissions and other economic incentives (Australian Bureau of Statistics 1995). Men are more likely than women to attain senior status and prestige (for example Cameron *et al.* 1995) and more likely to follow unbroken and successful career trajectories (for example Leonard 1996).

This inequity is largely maintained by the socially constructed necessity for women to leave the paid workforce in order to care for children. Girls are more successful than boys at school (Social Trends 1995) and are more likely to complete undergraduate degrees (Australian Bureau of Statistics 1995). But by the age of 30, men and women's career paths have clearly diverged, with at least some men moving into higher status and managerial positions and women tending to move down or leave the paid labour force (Rindfuss *et al.* 1999).

It is worth stressing the obvious point that there is nothing immutable or inevitable about these gender-based life trajectories; rather, they are a consequence of artificially constructed employment systems and government policies regarding parental leave and child support. These structural factors make it exceptionally difficult for both partners to maintain their employment patterns when they become parents. Then, gender-based expectations combine with the nature of an employment system that ensures that men are generally paid more than women, to mean that couples generally choose that the man will continue in his employment once he becomes a father. In fact, new fathers will usually work longer paid hours, while new mothers will work fewer or no paid hours (Bittman and Lovejoy 1993).

It is certainly the case that the majority of men do have full-time paid employment. Australian census data, which are typical of information on employment patterns in developed countries, indicate that 90 per cent of married men with children participate in the paid workforce (Australian Bureau of Statistics 1995), while the figure for married women with children under 15 is 40 per cent, and 80 per cent for women without children. In Britain in 1995, 70 per cent of men and 53 per cent of women of working age were in the paid workforce (Social Trends 1995). However, while men are still more likely than women to have full-time permanent employment, a significant proportion do not. The Australian Bureau of Statistics (1995) found that 7 per cent of all employed men worked part time and 16 per cent were in casual jobs. While this is significantly lower than the comparable figures of 39 per cent and 31 per cent respectively for women, it still represents a substantial proportion of employed men.

The psychological literature has been slow to acknowledge that there have been massive changes in employment patterns in the past few decades. Modern urban society is characterized by long-term unemployment, casualization of the workforce, decreased leisure time, high rates of family breakup and an increasing range of household structures (for example US Bureau of Labor Statistics 1991). The myth of the nuclear family, and the concept that a 'real man' supports a wife and children financially through a full-time permanent career outside the home, have become untenable for many people but continue to influence both men's and women's concepts of successful masculinity (Coltrane 1989).

Men continue to be socialized to see their careers as the most important aspect of their lives and to play a minimal or secondary role in domestic labour and childcare; the conflict between social expectations and the reality of personal and family lives leads to stress and to stress-related illness (for example Kahne 1991; Lundberg 1996). Men who do not conform to this stereotype are stigmatized and often find it difficult to avoid internalizing a perception of low self-esteem (for example Willott and Griffin 1997; Smith 1998); while it is well acknowledged that the job market has contracted, there still seems to be a widespread assumption that men without full-time permanent employment are somehow responsible for their circumstances. Pritchard (1992) showed that suicide rates among young men in Europe during the 1970s and 1980s were statistically associated with unemployment rates, and suggested that systemic unemployment appeared to have a differentially powerful effect on suicide among men of working age.

Social and government rhetoric still proclaims that a 'real' man will somehow go out and find a job whatever the circumstances, shifting the blame for unemployment to the individual, rather than exploring strategies for restructuring the workforce in acknowledgement of global changes in economic systems. In Australia, for example, a recent survey showed that the total amount of unpaid overtime worked by employees would, if converted into paid jobs, more than compensate for the total level of unemployment in that country (Hamilton and Denniss 2000). Further, this survey showed that the majority of employees who put in extra unpaid time were not doing this out of a personal commitment to their work, but did so because of a perception that they would risk losing their jobs if they did not.

Modern labour relations policies that emphasize short-term contracts and lack of employment security combine with social expectations to produce a system in which full-time, permanent paid jobs are increasingly scarce and increasingly demanding. While a radical restructure of employment systems would be required to change this, it is worth pointing out that all social systems are to some degree arbitrary. High levels of unemployment exist as a result of policy decisions, not for any immutable reason.

The majority of research on employment and well-being among men assumes that a man has, and should have, a full-time job and an otherwise unoccupied, female, housebound partner who maintains his home and deals with all other aspects of his life, leaving him completely free to concentrate on paid employment. The few exceptions to this (for example Duxbury and Higgins 1994; Milkie and Peltola 1999) generally find that men do indeed experience role conflicts between paid work and domestic responsibilities, particularly if they are fathers. Generally the level of conflict is lower than that experienced by women and tends to arise at a higher level of responsibility and commitment in the paid job (for example Greenglass *et al.* 1988). Extent of job control and decision latitude has been found to ameliorate role conflicts among both men and women (for example Rosenfield 1989; Piechowski 1992). Since men are more likely to attain senior career positions with a high level of self-determination, and are also likely to have fewer responsibilities and more discretion over their unpaid labour in the home, the ability to combine their paid work with the rest of their lives may be easier. Nevertheless, the majority of men will never reach senior positions or have discretion over their employment conditions, and thus a significant number of men are likely to experience high levels of role conflict.

The dearth of research on men's multiple roles is explicable by cultural stereotypes about legitimate male activities and therefore about what research is worth conducting. The neglect of the psychological impact of unemployment and underemployment, on the other hand, is somewhat less easy to explain. It may arise from an assumption among psychologists that unemployed men are individually responsible for their failure to find employment, and thus that it is simply laziness or intransigence, rather than anything that needs to be theorized and understood, that underlies men's failure to find work in a shrinking job market. What little research has been conducted on this topic suggests that men do indeed find it difficult to deal with a life in which their reason for existence is not full-time work outside the home. Further, this problem is confounded by findings that the women from whom they might expect social support also seem to internalize these stereotypes, and that their negative reactions serve to exacerbate men's distress (Davis 1993; Dixon 1998).

Dixon (1998), for example, in a study of the effects of systemic unemployment among African Americans, found that women, whether employed or unemployed themselves, expressed an expectation that a 'real man' would have a paid job, and tended to regard their unemployed husbands and friends as lazy, rather than as the victims of a radically altered economic environment. Dixon also found that men found it more difficult than women to cope personally with the same levels of unemployment and financial uncertainty, at least in part because men seem to internalize an assumption that there is a necessary relationship between masculinity and paid employment. As in other research, the men identified themselves primarily as workers and experienced a sense of loss of identity without a paid job, while the women identified themselves in terms of their relationships with family members and were better able to find a sense of identity other than in paid work.

In another detailed exploration of a particular society undergoing radical change, Davis (1993) explored gender relations in Newfoundland. Traditionally, there has been a strongly gender-based division of labour, with men spending long periods of time offshore on fishing boats and women working mainly without pay to maintain their homes. However, overfishing and economic changes have meant that commercial fishing is no longer viable in Newfoundland. Davis described a situation in which men were forced to 'invade' the traditionally female space of the land and involve themselves in traditionally female tasks. She described this change as resulting in a pervasive gender antagonism that dominated social and personal relationships, to the detriment of the emotional health of both men and women.

Lobo and Watkins (1995), in Australia, examined unemployment among middle-aged and older men, and found that even when wives were supportive, unemployed husbands generally found the role change hard to accept, especially if their wives had paid work. Women also had frequently internalized expectations about male- and female-appropriate work: many wives actively resisted their husbands' attempts to alter longstanding gender-based divisions of domestic labour by taking on 'women's work' within the home, and reported a sense of resentment that their husbands were no longer living up to what they regarded as 'their side of the bargain'. As the men's period of unemployment lengthened, wives became more critical, children became embarrassed by their fathers' perceived failure, and men's sense of self-blame increased. Family relationships were described as increasingly characterized by intolerance and nitpicking.

Thus, despite initial support and a recognition that the unemployment had arisen from factors outside the men's control, men and their families seem to find it difficult to avoid a sense that unemployment is a demonstration of the individual man's failure to meet social and personal expectations. If family members are unable to avoid stigmatizing attitudes to the unemployed men in their lives, it is unsurprising that psychological researchers have also failed to see unemployment as a legitimate issue in men's lives, and one in need of investigation.

Research is frequently conducted from a perspective that, either implicitly or explicitly, blames individual men for being unable to cope with social change, and fails to reflect on the effect of structural changes on employment opportunities. It also generally fails to take into account the role of paid employment in 'doing gender' for men. Expectations conveyed culturally, through media and literature, children's toys, and the assumptions of family and teachers, mean that boys grow up expecting to be employed and to regard employment as evidence of successful manhood. Thus, one reason why men seem to find unemployment harder to deal with than women (Dixon 1998) is that not having a paid job is transgressive for men in a way that it is not for women.

The negative effects of men's unemployment on their emotional health and on their intimate relationships appear to be mediated both by men's gender-based expectations for themselves, and by women's gender-based expectations for the men in their lives. This suggests a need for a radical realignment of the expectations of both men and women. The acceptance at an individual level of a wider range of alternatives in men's relationships with the paid workforce, and at a structural level of more flexibility and variation in work practices, could have a significant impact on men's emotional health and on the quality of their intimate relationships.

Domestic labour

The assumption that unpaid domestic labour is naturally women's work and that it is inferior to men's work might appear, like many other social arrangements, to be unproblematically beneficial to men. Certainly this assumption is not beneficial to women, who take on a higher burden of unpaid domestic work regardless of their paid employment status (Baxter and Bittman 1995). But it should not be assumed that cultural practices that are harmful to women are necessarily beneficial to all, or indeed any, men. The nineteenth-century concept of 'separate spheres', that men are naturally and essentially fit for public life and paid employment while women are equally naturally designed for the private world of home and family (Cott 1977), continues to restrict the choices of both men and women. In a society in which men cannot necessarily expect to find or maintain paid employment, and in which wives' and mothers' incomes are necessary to provide adequate living standards in many families, these patriarchal assumptions about paid and unpaid labour conflict with economic and social reality, and the benefits of these assumptions are by no means available to all men.

As is the case for paid work, there is a detailed psychological literature examining women's unpaid domestic work. This literature tends to be predicated on the assumption that women will necessarily take on paid work in addition to, and as a secondary role to, full responsibility for care of children and management of a home (Apter 1993). There is no parallel body of work that examines men's health and its relationship with their unpaid work commitments. Role conflicts are defined as a 'women's problem' and the social and cultural arrangements that support their asymmetry along gender lines are rendered invisible.

Perhaps the most well-established and culturally consistent research finding on gender and labour is that unpaid domestic labour is predominantly a female activity. When individuals move into domestic relationships, men's domestic labour tends to decrease while women's increases (Bittman and Lovejoy 1993; Gupta 1999). In a comparison of five western developed countries – USA, Sweden, Norway, Canada and Australia – Baxter (1997) found few differences in the extent to which women took on the majority of unpaid domestic work. Similarly, Wright *et al.* (1992) found equal levels of inequity in dual-earner couples in the USA and Sweden, regardless of social class. This is despite major differences between countries at the public policy level in gender relations, for example in conditions for parental leave and in regulations which aim to prevent restrictions on paid work on the basis of gender. A comparison of data from Indonesia, the Philippines, Taiwan, South Korea and the USA (Sanchez 1993), surprisingly, also found few differences in the distribution of domestic labour. Material conditions, national development and public policy appear to play a limited role in inequity at the level of domestic labour (Sanchez 1993; Baxter 1997).

Decisions about, and the conduct of, domestic labour are women's work by default. Despite egalitarian attitudes to domestic labour among most working couples (Bittman and Lovejoy 1993), both the magnitude and the specifics of actual workload are still strongly affected by social expectations about gender-appropriate responsibilities (Greenglass 1991; Perry-Jenkins 1993). Surveys from a number of different countries, using a range of different methodologies (Blair and Lichter 1991; Bittman 1992; South and Spitze 1994; Social Trends 1995), are consistent in showing that women carry out more unpaid domestic labour than men, and that the division of that labour tends to be on sex-based lines, with women taking responsibility for cooking, cleaning and childcare while men predominate in home and car maintenance, gardening and outside chores. Even when wives spend more hours in paid work than their husbands, they still do far more unpaid domestic work than men: Ishii-Kuntz and Coltrane (1992) found that husbands in such households carried out 26 per cent of the childcare and 21 per cent of the housework.

Most men seem to internalize a view that they have a responsibility to provide financially for their families, and that other forms of provision or support are not part of their role as husband and father (Perry-Jenkins and Crouter 1990). Women, by contrast, are socialized to view caring for others and maintaining a household as at least as valuable a contribution to their family and to society as is providing financially (Perry-Jenkins 1993). Women tend to see domestic labour as their responsibility, while men are more likely to see their contributions to domestic labour as 'helping out' (Gunter and Gunter 1990).

Men's attitudes to domestic work appear to have little to do with their participation unless their female partners are prepared to raise it as an issue of equity. 'Husbands do relatively little domestic labour unless both they and their wives are relatively egalitarian in their beliefs about gender and marital roles' (Bittman and Lovejoy 1993: 585). Men, to at least some extent, cope with the ambiguities of domestic labour by ignoring the problem as much as possible.

There is ample evidence from several countries that perceived equity in division of domestic labour is an important predictor of relationship satisfaction (for example Wilkie *et al.* 1998). Perceptions of equity are different for men and for women (Wilkie *et al.* 1998), but both men and women seem to accept an objectively inequitable division of labour as both fair and reasonable, and to regard domestic labour as primarily the woman's responsibility. Women are more likely than men to take on the supervision and planning roles, while men's contributions to domestic labour are popularly construed as 'helping'. The notion that men have any role at all in domestic labour is a relatively recent one; Segal (1990), for example, has described gender relations in the 1950s as hinging on expectations about domestic roles that are essentially no different from the nineteenth-century concept of 'separate spheres'.

Differences in men's and women's relationships with unpaid domestic labour, and acceptance that it is 'natural' for men to contribute less than women, have strong historical roots and are inextricably connected with gendered meanings which are attached to both paid and unpaid work. The relationship between actual hours of work, the nature of that work, and the degree of satisfaction or discontent in men and women is not straightforward.

As for paid labour, the majority of gender-based research on unpaid domestic labour focuses on women and their perspectives; men's attitudes and the extent to which they perceive inequities have not received the same attention. Women are, in general, more contented with inequitable division of labour than might be expected. Major (1993) has argued that this arises from a gendered society that has produced men who feel they have more entitlement to leisure than do women, and women who compare their lives with other women and with cultural and media-presented stereotypes of what constitutes 'normal' domestic life, rather than with the men with whom they live. Factors affecting women's sense of justice in domestic labour include the extent to which a woman has other, more valued, things to do with her time, her tendency to use within- or between-gender comparisons in deciding what is 'fair', and the extent to which she is willing to endorse sexist excuses for men's taking a lower workload (Thompson 1991).

Kroska (1997) has argued that widespread satisfaction with objective inequities in domestic labour needs to be understood in the context of 'doing gender'. Members of a relationship prefer to contribute to that relationship in ways which reflect their personal and gender identity. Thus, they will choose types and amounts of activities which are congruent with their sense of self, including their gender identity. In a sexist society, men are less likely to feel comfortable in childcare and cleaning; thus, they will often find it easier to leave the majority of domestic work to be done by their partner, perhaps justifying this by invocation of cultural stereotypes of men's domestic incapacity or lower standards of domestic hygiene, than to find ways of making a fair contribution to their households (Greenglass 1991; Bittman 1992).

This argument suggests that a more equitable approach to unpaid labour requires a fundamental cultural change, not a blaming of individual men for being lazy or unappreciative, but a change in cultural perceptions of what being a man is all about.

Again, gender stereotypes of men are internalized both by men and by women. A corollary of the cultural basis to the division of unpaid labour is that at least some women appear to take active steps to exclude men from participation in domestic labour. Again this may be interpreted, not as individual perverseness, but as women attempting to 'do gender' in a changing social world. Allen and Hawkins (1999), for example, presented evidence that at least some women (21 per cent of a sample of American dual-earner couples) were reluctant to relinquish their traditional responsibility for, and control over, the domestic sphere. These women, it was argued, were seeking some control and status in the feminine-typed aspects of their lives, even at the cost of highly inequitable unpaid domestic labour workloads on top of paid employment.

Gender-based inequities in workloads are often explained solely by individual attitudes and choices. Research such as that of Grbich (1992, 1995) with role-reversed households demonstrates that it is possible for individual couples to come to their own idiosyncratic arrangements for the allocation of household labour. However, broader structural aspects of society and of paid work put constraints on the organization of most individuals' times. In Britain, for example, 62 per cent of couples said that they believed that housework should be divided equally, but only 27 per cent actually achieved this equity (Social Trends 1995). Thus, it can be argued that efforts to deal with the problem of women's workloads will be unsuccessful if they focus only on individual men and women, and assume that their choices about time use and the division of labour are always made freely and on an individual basis.

The equation of domestic labour with femininity is culturally reinforced at many levels. Grbich (1992) found that men who took on the primary caregiver role experienced strong negative reactions from their peers, who conveyed a sense that the role was simply not appropriate for Australian men and that, by transgressing an important social precept, these men were letting their mates down. This gender-role stereotyping is apparent from an early age: even children are allocated household tasks along gender lines, and at all ages girls have more household tasks than boys (Mauldin and Meeks 1990; Blair 1992). Analyses of media images of families and households, and particularly advertisements for household products, childcare products and food and cooking products, have demonstrated an equation of domestic labour with femininity in both western and Asian cultures (Coltrane and Adams 1997; Furnham *et al*. 2000). If men are ever portrayed engaging in domestic labour they are generally doing it badly, with a bad grace, or at the very least with an elegant sense of irony. Men who are competent in household management or food preparation are overwhelmingly portrayed as homosexual, and thus as outside the mainstream and not to be taken seriously as models of 'appropriate' masculine behaviour.

Domestic labour appears to be another area in which traditional and contemporary concepts of masculinity conflict. The socialization processes which discourage men from developing skills or interest in domestic labour are contradicted by the value which is placed on a non-sexist and egalitarian approach to relationships, leaving men (and women) in the uncomfortable situation in which they must negotiate individual household arrangements, but in which the conflicting nature of cultural prescriptions means any choice will be in some sense wrong. Research (for example Bittman and Lovejoy 1993) shows that many couples deal with this ambiguity by maintaining unequal work practices despite a verbal commitment to equity. While a small number of couples do appear able to divide housework and childcare equitably (Risman and Johnson-Sumerford 1998), this is by no means easy and a much larger number of couples live with less equity than they claim they would prefer (for example Voydanoff and Donnelly 1999). Again, it is of limited value to attribute this to individual men's intransigence or women's gullibility, and it is more useful to consider this as a creative strategy by which individual couples deal with the conflicting demands placed on them by cultural expectations.

Men, women, work and relationships

Evidence (for example Bird 1999) that inequities in household labour go some way to explaining the higher levels of depression among women suggests that men might also benefit in a more equitable system if their partners were happier. Arguments such as these, though, are opposed by research which appears to support a zero-sum model of human happiness, suggesting that benefits which accrue to women from equitable family circumstances must be at the expense of men. For example, Rosenfield (1992) found that women's paid employment had a negative effect on their husbands' mental health, and that this effect was correlated with the extent that it reduced income disparity and increased the men's unpaid domestic workloads – two factors which contribute positively to women's mental health. Data from the 1970s and 1980s in the USA and Canada (Krull and Trovato 1994; Burr *et al*. 1997) has even suggested that changes from traditional gender-based work patterns and increased participation of mothers in the paid workforce may have been positively related to male suicide. More recent evidence (for example Burr *et al*. 1997) suggests that this effect has disappeared, suggesting that it may have been the process of change that was disturbing for men, rather than women's paid work *per se*.

It has also been argued that increases in wives' incomes may increase marital discord by shifting the power balance within relationships. However, Rodgers (1999) has demonstrated that any association is more likely to be the reverse, an effect of marital discord on women's employment patterns. Women in unsatisfactory relationships are more likely than other women to seek paid work, either in order to obtain alternative sources of personal satisfaction or out of a concern to maintain a level of independence and choice for their future lives.

It is unhelpful, however, to take this as evidence for the view that men must suffer if women are to receive fair treatment. The assumption that improvements in women's circumstances are inevitably negative for men is part of the unfounded rhetoric of social conservatives whose aim is to reinforce an antagonistic relationship between men's and women's concerns, and is neither helpful to the development of a more egalitarian society nor the only interpretation which can be placed on these data. Rather, it may be more useful to interpret these findings as arising from the fact that employment continues to be structured on the assumption that a worker will have an unpaid domestic assistant, so that men whose female partners are in paid work find it difficult to manage their time. Such an interpretation leads logically to the view that changes in employment structures might be beneficial to the health and well-being of both men and women.

Psychological research has generally failed to explore the cultural basis of these data, and continues to be based on outdated and increasingly untenable social assumptions. For example, Olds *et al.* (1993), in a paper which purported to examine the effects of part-time employment and shared childcare on parents' well-being, in fact studied couples in which the woman worked part time and the man full time. The researchers, presumably, assumed that men did not work part time. Again, Koch *et al.* (1991) examined the coping strategies that US women used to juggle the stress of work and home commitments, and suggested the need for stress management for those women, but failed to mention the possibility that men might also encounter role conflicts or stresses, or that a change in the division of labour might be more effective in reducing the women's stress and possibly improving their male partners' lives at the same time. These examples are typical of a large body of literature which fails to examine the assumptions we make, both about the work involvement of men and women, and about the structure of work environments.

Childcare

Some researchers separate childcare from other unpaid domestic labour in analysing the relative contributions of men and women. People generally find childcare more enjoyable than cleaning and housework, and fathers who do contribute to household labour are more likely to involve themselves with childcare than with other tasks (for example Deutsch *et al.* 1993). Two Australian studies (Baxter *et al.* 1991; Baxter and Bittman 1995) have shown that, despite this preference, men still spent significantly less time than women in childcare, with average weekly involvement being between 13 and 18 hours for mothers and between 3 and 8 hours for fathers. By contrast, a Canadian study (Hannah and Quarter 1992) demonstrated a reasonably equitable division of childcare labour, with mothers still taking a far greater responsibility for all other work. Men in role-reversed households (Grbich 1995) reported that they enjoyed childcare and happily took on most of those aspects of domestic work. By contrast, they disliked housework, seeing it as boring, repetitive and unfulfilling. While women in these households did very little housework, averaging little more than men in traditional households, they were still most likely to take on the cleaning of floors, bathrooms and toilets.

The assumption that men are fundamentally less able than women to look after children (for example Hojat 1990) can be traced to essentialist views about the nature of men and of women and the widely believed myth of the 'mothering instinct'. There is, however, no evidence that men are unable to provide adequate childcare. Feminist writers (for example Badinter 1981; Rich 1982; Wearing 1984) have pointed out that the assumption that only women can care for children has the effect of restricting women's choices and their economic and social power. Simultaneously, it denies the validity of men's interest in, and concern for, their own children. It serves to exclude men from emotional closeness and caring activities within their families (Carrigan *et al.* 1985) and in a time when men may be less able to construct personal identities through paid work, it reduces their capacity to construct a positive identity through fatherhood.

Because of the dominance of the traditional view of a man's role in his family as that of the largely absent breadwinner, many men who might prefer a more active role in their families have little idea of their role in childcare (for example Jordan 1990). Parents find it difficult to avoid the traditional division of labour even if they have strong intentions to do so (for example Reichle and Gefke 1998).

There is evidence that men's active involvement in family life tends to lead to better relationships with their partners and children (for example Hawkins *et al.* 1993; Bailey 1994) and in particular to better emotional outcomes for their sons (Brody 1999). However, even those fathers with a strong personal commitment to parenting seem to become involved only when their partners' employment schedules require it. Both broader social structures and individual gender socialization make an equitable approach to parenting and to household labour extremely difficult to put into practice (Smith 1998). As a result, many parents, both fathers and mothers, internalize traditional notions about fatherhood and motherhood, endorsing the view that women should play the major parenting roles and that men should provide supervised assistance when asked; Dempsey (2000) found this to be the case even when the women were also in full-time employment.

The assumption that the work of childcare is self-evidently women's work is reflected in the psychological literature. For example, a survey of infant care in dual-earner couples examined the circumstances under which mothers would engage in 'substituting fathers for paid child-care providers' (Glass 1998: 821), the wording suggesting that the researcher holds a worldview that categorizes the notion of fathers caring for their own children as deviant, as less appropriate than paying to have them cared for by a stranger, and as in need of investigation.

In some families where childcare is shared by both parents, the parents carry out psychological work in order to maintain the man's sense of himself as the breadwinner. Deutsch and Saxon (1998) conducted in-depth interviews with US working-class couples who worked alternate shifts and shared the care of their children. These couples managed to maintain traditional gender beliefs, despite living an egalitarian lifestyle, by maintaining the perception that the father was the breadwinner and the one with the 'real' job; the mother was still the central caregiver, and worked only because of financial pressures, which were frequently constructed as temporary. In this way, these couples actively constructed a view of their family life that conflicted with their material circumstances but not with traditional, essentialist concepts of appropriate male and female behaviour. This example demonstrates the strength of cultural stereotypes, the psychological discomfort involved in challenging them at an individual level, and the lengths to which people will go to reduce this discomfort.

It also provides an interesting contrast with the evidence presented earlier (for example Bittman and Lovejoy 1993), describing couples who maintain a verbal commitment to egalitarian household management while dividing actual household labour inequitably. Both these arrangements can be seen as strategies for reconciling inconsistent cultural prescriptions on men and women, to be simultaneously traditional and egalitarian.

Non-traditional household structures

The small amount of psychological research which has focused on the health outcomes associated with paid and unpaid work for men is predicated on the assumption that men are heterosexual and live in partnerships with women. The strategies which gay men, and men living in other non-traditional circumstances, use to negotiate paid and unpaid labour would provide information on alternative social and personal arrangements. Men who do not live in traditional nuclear families are forced to make active decisions about many aspects of their lives, including the allocation of unpaid domestic labour.

The experiences of these men are of interest in their own right, but may also provide models of more egalitarian relationship structures for other men. There is, however, very little research which surveys same-sex households without problematizing them; an exception is the work of Kurdek (1993), who found that members of same-sex households had more equitable division of labour than did heterosexual couples. In general, Kurdek found that male couples tended to divide the tasks between individuals, each choosing the ones he preferred, while lesbian couples were more likely to share tasks. While such research is of value in that it legitimizes non-traditional household structures, there is a need for work that explores the conflicts and compromises made by men who live in gay relationships or other non-traditional household relationships in the negotiation of responsibility for domestic labour. More generally, the lives and concerns of these men have received little attention; focus has instead been very narrowly on issues of sexual health or psychopathology, rather than more broadly on gay men's lives, relationships and positions in society (Clark 1995), again problematizing gay men rather than exploring their lifestyles as legitimate alternative choices and tackling issues of homophobia and discrimination (Kirby 2000).

It is estimated that 2 per cent of US households are completely role reversed, with a woman in full-time paid work and a man taking care of unpaid domestic work (US Bureau of the Census 1993). Smith (1998), in a qualitative study of 11 Australian fathers in role-reversed relationships, found that the men found their role difficult, both to define and to carry out. The men lacked confidence in their ability to carry out domestic tasks, particularly childcare, and appeared to believe that being male made them necessarily less capable parents than the 'other mothers'.

They described difficulties in establishing the legitimacy of their role; for example, mothers at crèche assumed that the fathers were temporarily in charge while the 'real' carer was otherwise engaged. Their daily lives were also made more difficult by material and structural manifestations of the gender order, such as the positioning of baby changing rooms in women's toilets and the provision of social events for parents which explicitly excluded fathers (ladies' tennis, mothers' groups). Some men reported that simply being a man alone with a baby was enough to elicit concerned reactions from strangers.

These men used a number of strategies to cope with their lifestyle, which had usually arisen unintentionally because they had been unable to find paid work. They felt that the situation had pushed them to re-evaluate previously accepted notions of masculinity, specifically to reject traditional views of essential differences between the sexes, and were generally positive about undergoing what they saw as a significant developmental process, but still reported an overall sense of isolation, difficulty and role illegitimacy.

Similarly, the work of Grbich (1992), also with role-reversed parents in Australia, indicated that fathers had to deal with strong negative reactions from their social group, and a sense that the role of primary caregiver was not an appropriate one for men. These men reported that, over time, their own attitudes and behaviours and those of their wives shifted towards a more egalitarian view of roles and responsibilities, and again they generally described these changes in positive terms (Grbich 1995). This illustration of the well-known effect of exposure in increasing positive attitudes (Zimbardo and Leippe 1991) suggests that men's negative attitudes to domestic labour are subject to change through experience.

Conclusion

It is clear that men are socialized to see paid work as of central importance in their lives, in their definitions of themselves, and in their sense of self-worth. Given the centrality of working to men's sense of self, there is surprisingly little psychological research on the extent to which patterns of paid and unpaid work, and discrepancies between desired and actual patterns of employment, affect men's physical and emotional health. This is particularly a concern given the structural changes in patterns of employment. Increasingly, men need to juggle the traditional view that a real man provides financially for his family with contemporary definitions of masculinity which emphasize egalitarianism and flexibility, in the context of rapid changes to work and family structures.

The challenge for men is to find new ways of defining themselves and their sense of self-worth other than exclusively through paid work. The advantages which may accrue to men who are able to view their identity in a more relational and less instrumental light are explored in the next chapter, which focuses on men and their families.

Summary

- Cultural stereotypes continue to define men primarily by their paid employment, and to treat their contributions to unpaid domestic labour as secondary and optional.
- Systemic changes to the employment systems mean that full-time employment is less readily available than it was a generation ago, yet men who are unable to find paid work are stigmatized and held individually responsible.
- Psychology is almost entirely silent on the issues surrounding paid work and unemployment for men; this may be because mainstream psychology assumes that finding a paid job is simply a matter of making a personal effort, and fails to acknowledge systemic influences which limit individual opportunity.
- Men throughout the world undertake considerably less unpaid domestic labour than their female partners, regardless of the amount of paid work carried out by those women.

- While both men and women claim that they believe unpaid labour should be divided equitably within the household, both men and women appear happy with objectively inequitable workloads.
- This paradox has not been the subject of psychological research.
- While childcare is generally preferred to other aspects of domestic labour, men's contributions in this area are also less than women's.
- When men do involve themselves in childcare, there are measurable benefits to them, their partners and their children; yet mainstream psychology continues to treat men's involvement with the rearing of their children as deviant or problematic.
- Men in contemporary society are caught in a structural dilemma between traditional expectations that their identity is defined by paid work, and contemporary ideals of gender equity; whatever choices they and their partners make regarding the balance of labour, men will transgress some cultural expectations.
- While a minority of men live in non-traditional households, including gay relationships and role-reversed households, there is little research which examines the viability of these lifestyles; thus, traditional family structures are treated as necessary and normal.

Additional reading

Coltrane, S. (1989) Household labour and the routine production of gender, *Social Problems*, 36: 473–90.
Smith, C.D. (1998) 'Men don't do this sort of thing': a case study of the social isolation of househusbands, *Men and Masculinities*, 1: 138–72.
Willott, S. and Griffin, C. (1997) 'Wham bam, am I a man?': unemployed men talk about masculinities, *Feminism and Psychology*, 7: 107–28.

Men and family

Chapter 7 argued that hegemonic masculinity defines men according to their formal paid jobs, and that this is problematic not only because changes in employment patterns make this prescribed role harder to maintain, but also because this rigid definition reduces men's capacity to choose to be actively involved in family life. Many men who would prefer a more active role in their families have little idea of how to achieve this, and whatever their spoken preferences, families find it difficult to avoid the traditional division of labour, despite evidence that this reduces the quality of men's relationships with partners and children (for example Hawkins *et al.* 1993).

This chapter reviews evidence on the roles of men in families, focusing on men as fathers and on the effects on men of relationship breakdown. Changes in social structures mean that men's family experiences are increasingly central to their identities. This chapter, like the last, points to the asymmetries between expectations for men and for women. It also points to the contradictions between traditional patriarchal expectations for men and contemporary egalitarian expectations for couples. In the family as in the workforce, men are caught in a structural dilemma in which any choice will be less than ideal. Once again, however, stereotypes of appropriate gender-based behaviours and interests appear to have influenced mainstream research agendas. Thus, mothering and motherhood have been subjected to intense scrutiny while with few exceptions (for example Thomas 1994) the parenting experiences of men have been largely ignored.

Contemporary psychological theorists generally reject models (for example Deutsch 1947; Bowlby 1951) that explicitly adopt, and treat as self-evidently true, the unsubstantiated social myths which underlie essentialist models of gender difference: myths such as men's inability to provide childcare and women's psychological need for parenthood. But the psychological literature continues to be based on an implicit assumption that men's relationships with their families are peripheral and largely unnecessary, and that any male role in the family can just as easily be taken by anyone else with the requisite chromosomes (Phares 1999). The asymmetries inherent in psychology's perspectives on men's and women's roles in their families are illustrated in a variety of ways. Critical psychologists (for example Caplan and Hall-McCorquodale 1985; Phares 1992) have comprehensively deconstructed the assumption that mothers are entirely responsible for children's successful development, and for their emotional and behavioural problems, and have initiated programmes of research which explore the role of fathering in children's emotional health (for example Phares 1999).

Less well documented, and less openly explored, have been the asymmetries which underlie other imbalances in the psychological literature. There exists a large and well-articulated literature on the vicissitudes of women who need to combine paid work with essential caring roles in their homes (for example Doress-Worters 1994) and an even larger one which addresses the emotional difficulties associated with the difficult transition to motherhood (for example Lee 1997). The parallel literatures focusing on the reality of men's multiple work and family roles, caregiving and parenthood are small and fragmented, and to be found mainly in small specialist journals which do not command the same centrality in the psychological literature. The psychological mainstream does not in general recognize these as legitimate concerns, because family issues are not situated as a legitimate concern for men.

This chapter addresses the psychological issues arising for men in relation to their families, and illustrates the need for more, and more theoretically driven, research in areas which impinge on the emotional well-being of men as well as on the lives of their partners and children.

Fatherhood

Men, like women, generally grow up with the expectation that they will have children (Grewal and Urschel 1994; Willén 1994). Webb and Daniluk (1999), in a study of infertile men, described these men's view of fatherhood: that fatherhood was a natural part of being an adult man, a right and a cultural tradition that they, in common with men in general, looked forward to carrying on in their own lives. Conservative social commentators (for example Popenoe 1993) have deplored what they see as a loss of interest in family life at social, cultural, political and personal levels, emerging from an increasing proportion of unmarried mothers and of marital breakdowns, but there is little hard evidence to suggest that men are not interested in fatherhood and in the responsibilities and rewards which accompany it. Although births outside formal marriage have increased in recent years, it is still the case that over 95 per cent of new mothers have a male partner (Australian Bureau of Statistics 1995) and that, despite rhetoric about absent fathers, the majority of men have positive views about fatherhood and family life.

Yet, despite this pervasive social attitude that fatherhood is both natural and desirable, it has not been positioned as central to men's identities in the same way that motherhood is equated with adult womanhood (National Health and Medical Research Council of Australia (NHMRC) 1995). Coltrane (1995) has argued that contemporary social changes are leading to positive changes in fathers' involvement in family life; he sees increased and better paid employment opportunities for women, and a breakdown in the rigid and hierarchical nature of family structures and of gender attitudes, as producing men who are less concerned about fulfilling the breadwinner role, more involved in family life, and characterized by more balanced and positive self-identities. This optimistic view is contrasted with research demonstrating that contemporary fathers, despite positive attitudes, often have difficulty identifying their role (Jordan 1990; Lupton and Barclay 1997). Fatherhood is a domain in which conflicts between traditional and contemporary constructions of masculinity have the potential to cause considerable distress.

Social discourses for fathers continue to be conflictual; while contemporary social discourses place value on fathers who are actively involved in caring for their children, there continues to be a deeply ingrained cultural perception that men's primary role is as material providers, and that men are inevitably less competent as nurturing parents than women (Jordan 1990; Perry-Jenkins 1993). Even if explicit attempts are made to share the work of childcare equally, there is still a perception that the mother will 'naturally' know what to do: she will take charge and the father will help or follow her lead (for example Walzer 1996).

Fathers, therefore, often find themselves in a structural dilemma, with no possibility of making a choice which will be optimal for themselves, their partners and their relationships with friends, family, workmates and their broader social environment. Men may plan to be actively involved as parents, but find that carrying out their intentions is just too difficult, and this can lead to stress and disappointment for them as well as for their partners (Nicolson 1990).

It is frequently argued (for example Hawkins *et al.* 1993) that a closer involvement by fathers in the parenting process would lead to more positive personal development among men, as well as a closer match between men's and women's adult life trajectories, which might serve to maintain the quality of their marital relationship. A study of Dutch families (Kalmijn 1999) found that fathers who were more involved in childrearing generally had happier and more stable marriages, and that this effect appeared to be mediated by the finding that wives of involved fathers were happier. In Israel, Levy-Skiff (1994) has shown that the extent of the father's involvement in both play and caregiving with his child is a good predictor of marital satisfaction for both parents. Children, too, appreciate involved fathers: a study of US 8-year-olds who were asked to write essays about what made their father 'the best' (Milkie *et al.* 1997) found that the children wrote almost exclusively about their fathers' involvement in family life, caregiving and recreational activities, not about their paid jobs.

However, the work of Lupton and Barclay (1997), who conducted repeated interviews with Australian men during their transition to fatherhood, demonstrates that involved fatherhood is hardly a free and individual choice. Some men had internalized assumptions that childcare was 'women's work' which was inappropriate and demeaning for men, or that women had some magic innate knowledge about childcare from which men were excluded by virtue of their biology, and the idea that they should be involved in childcare was simply incompatible with their views of families and gender relations. Others recognized that these assumptions were cultural constructions, but still faced practical, employment-related and personal barriers which made this choice harder than the adoption of a gender-based division of labour; these men expressed a sense of discomfort with the way in which fatherhood had turned out for them, but could not see a practical way of arranging their lives differently.

Cultural arrangements which affect men's relationships with their children appear to be linked with other variables (Coltrane 1982). At a global level, societies in which men are closely involved in caring for their children also tend to be those in which men and women have more equal relationships; they are also characterized by low rates of aggressive and dominant behaviour among men, significant levels of female control over property, and an ideology of relative sexual egalitarianism. This suggests that relationships between men and their children are embedded in broader cultural assumptions about gender, power and social roles. In turn, this supports the view that individual men's choices about their day-to-day relationships with their children are to some extent constrained by sociocultural expectations, and the practical result of this is that some choices will be easier to make than others.

The decision to be an active and involved father is not, therefore, unproblematic. Lamb *et al.* (1986) have characterized it as having advantages and disadvantages for both father and mother. In choosing a model of fatherhood that conflicts with traditional cultural expectations, they argue, fathers stand to gain in emotional closeness, but may be disadvantaged in their careers and financial situation, aspects of life which are traditionally regarded as more central to traditional male self-identity; they may also experience relationship conflict as a result of their partner's uneasiness with changes in domestic roles (for example Lobo and Watkins 1995), their total workload may increase if childcare is added to paid employment, and they may experience social isolation or rejection by other men (for example Grbich 1992). Mothers, for their part, may see a reduction in their domestic labour at the expense of an increase in relationship conflicts and the loss of the exclusivity of the mother–child relationship. The relative weightings of these costs and benefits will depend on individuals' attitudes and values, but are also embedded in a social and cultural context.

Men who become fathers later in life seem more able to resist pressures to adopt traditional roles; Cooney *et al.* (1993) found that older fathers were more involved with their children and enjoyed fatherhood more. However, decisions about the timing of parenthood are confounded with educational level and social class, factors that also influence individuals' abilities to make decisions which are at odds with social expectations (Coltrane 1990).

An important predictor of fathers' involvement in childcare and family work, and their definitions of themselves as fathers and of fatherhood as a concept, is the type of relationship they had with their own fathers (Barnett and Baruch 1987; White 1994). This suggests that men's perceptions of the fathering role may be well established before they reach adulthood. In combination with the cultural influences which restrict individual choice regardless of preference, this means that changes in socially accepted fatherhood roles are unlikely to happen quickly.

In considering reasons why men might not take on an active fatherhood role, Pleck *et al.* (1986) have argued that this choice is multiply determined by a range of factors including a lack of motivation, lack of skills, lack of positive social support, and institutional and practical barriers such as the nature of the workplace and the need to provide financial support. Psychology, however, has been slow to recognize the extent to which cultural images of fatherhood (for example Coltrane and Allan 1994) influence men's individual choices and behaviours. Fatherhood roles may best be understood as determined by a combination of personal, social, structural and socialization factors. There is, however, considerable variation in how these influences are reproduced socially and culturally, and thus in the ease with which individuals can choose to reject or modify their influence. Psychology, where it has addressed fatherhood at all, has not considered these issues.

While research on fatherhood is beginning to appear in specialist books and journals, mainstream work on parenthood continues to ignore the role of fathers. There is remarkably little research that examines the emotional effects on men of becoming fathers, with the focus tending to be on the effect on children of the presence or absence of a father figure in the home (for example Clarke-Stewart *et al.* 2000); the impact on the individual man of fatherhood, or of the loss of a relationship with his children through relationship breakdown, has been largely ignored (Long 1997). The exceptions that exist are largely in two areas, that of postnatal depression, and that of the experiences of men whose expectations of fatherhood are not fulfilled as expected. Both of these literatures, however, are considerably smaller and less well developed than the literatures to which they are very obviously secondary, those on parallel experiences among women. While there is some extremely powerful man-centred research in both these areas, in general the reader cannot escape a sensation that research models and assumptions continue to focus on women's depression and women's fertility problems, and that men are included in the research more out of politeness than because of any sense that these experiences might be centrally relevant to men.

Mainstream psychological literature on the transition to motherhood is generally based on an assumption that the transition should be easy and unproblematically blissful. Motherhood is assumed to be both natural and the highest state to which a woman can aspire; thus, women who struggle with the difficult changes in lifestyle and responsibilities must have a psychiatric disorder, probably hormonally mediated. The extent to which this myth is maintained, despite the facts that there is no convincing evidence for a biological explanation of postpartum depression, while there is extensive support for social explanations (Kumar 1994), is testament to the strength of cultural beliefs about motherhood (Rich 1982). Lee (1997) has argued that the evidence suggests that the majority of parents, both fathers and mothers, find the transitions associated with new parenthood to be difficult, and that it is more reasonable to see postpartum depression as one end of a continuum of normal adjustment to major life change, and not as something qualitatively different from other new parents' experiences.

Perhaps the strongest evidence for this interpretation is evidence from clinical research that fathers, too, experience postpartum depression. Richman et al. (1991) found that fathers were as likely as mothers to be clinically depressed two months after the birth of a child; Ballard et al. (1994) found that 9 per cent of fathers were depressed six weeks after the birth, and 5 per cent were depressed at six months. Further, both mothers and fathers of children aged 3 to 5 had similar levels of depression to mothers and fathers of newborns, again suggesting that explanations of postpartum depression are more likely to be found in the continuing stresses of caring for a small child than in any exclusively female hormonal change associated with childbirth. The interconnections between the coping abilities of the two parents is demonstrated by the finding that fathers are at greatest risk of depression if their partners have received a diagnosis of depression (Lovestone and Kumar 1993; Ballard et al. 1994; Zelkowitz and Milet 1997). Fathers' adjustment problems, like mothers', are strongly related to lack of social support and high levels of economic and work-related pressure (Zelkowitz and Milet 1997).

This research, derived from traditional models of individual psychopathology, is consistent with findings from research using qualitative and reflexive methods (for example Lupton and Barclay 1997) in demonstrating the social pressures on new parents and the physical and emotional effects of the unexpectedly high workloads and sense of overwhelming responsibility. The consistency of research conclusions across such diverse research methods and epistemologies suggests that fathering is indeed a major life challenge and that a psychology that acknowledges the conflicting pressures on fathers has the potential to provide strategies to help men and their partners to cope better.

Fertility problems

Inability to conceive, at least temporarily, is a reasonably common problem among heterosexual couples, with estimates of its prevalence as high as one in six couples (Daniluk 1991). Infertility may arise from health problems of either or both partners (Valentine 1986), but both medical and psychological research on failure to conceive has focused almost exclusively on women (Rowland 1992). Lifestyle factors such as smoking and drinking have a greater effect on men's fertility (for example reducing sperm count and motility) than on women's (Florack *et al.* 1994). Yet there is no systematic research that explores the effects of men's lifestyles on their ability to father children. Treatment-seeking is nearly always initiated by the woman rather than the man (Webb and Daniluk 1999), and men generally do not undergo medical testing until after their partners have been thoroughly examined (Rowland 1992). These observations reflect a pervasive cultural perspective that parenthood and its precursors are essentially 'women's business', and that men should be less interested in infertility and less concerned if they and their partner do not conceive as quickly as they had expected.

The two main forms of treatment for infertility are artificial insemination (AI) and in vitro fertilization (IVF). AI is used when a man is infertile or has insufficient sperm for natural fertilization, but his female partner has no conception-related problems. Donor sperm, or a concentrated sample of the man's sperm, is introduced into his partner's vagina or uterus, and conception and implantation then occur naturally. IVF is used when the woman has biological problems which prevent natural conception or implantation; the term refers to a range of techniques which involve the removal of an ovum from the woman's body, or the use of a donor ovum, its fertilization in the laboratory using either the male partner's or a donor's sperm, and the later implantation of the resultant embryo in the woman's uterus.

AI has a success rate per treatment that varies between about 20 per cent (Horne *et al.* 1998) and 60 per cent (Ferrara *et al.* 2000); while this is significantly higher than the success rate of IVF (NHMRC 1995), it still means that infertile men can expect that they and their partners will need to undergo anything up to a dozen cycles of treatment, with associated emotional distress for both partners. The effects of unsuccessful treatment are negative for both men and women. While men and women entering treatment for infertility are generally psychologically healthy and have positive expectations of the treatment and its outcome (Connolly *et al.* 1992), stress increases and relationship quality decreases over the period of treatment (for example Benazon *et al.* 1992). Of course, adequate controls are as necessary here as in other areas, as it appears that relationship satisfaction also trends downwards in couples who are not seeking fertility treatment (Belsky and Pensky 1988).

There has been very little research that focuses on the psychological effects on men of infertility. Research on infertility focuses almost entirely on the woman who is trying to conceive, seeing the man's role as essentially supportive. One project which did focus on men's experiences of infertility (Webb and Daniluk 1999) found that the men consistently described experiences of grief, loss and shock that they could be infertile, coupled with a sense of powerlessness and inadequacy and of letting their partners down. The men felt isolated and confused, without any social models of what they might expect to experience or how they might react.

Another fertility-related area in which men's experiences have been almost entirely ignored is that of foetal loss through miscarriage. Miscarriage, or spontaneous abortion, is quite common, occurring in somewhere between 12 and 24 per cent of pregnancies (Schofield *et al.* 2000). While there is a limited amount of research dealing with women's reactions to miscarriage (Madden 1994; Bowles *et al.* 2000), the reactions of men have been almost completely ignored. Some exceptions are found in the work of Johnson and Puddifoot (Johnson and Puddifoot 1996; Puddifoot and Johnson 1997, 1999) and DeFrain *et al.* (1996), who have shown that men experience considerable distress following their partners' miscarriage, and that their grief is frequently exacerbated by confusion over appropriate behaviour. Similar levels of distress and confusion are experienced following a stillbirth (DeFrain *et al.* 1990).

Men at this time felt a strong need to be supportive to their partners, to the extent that they thought it necessary to deny their own need for support. They frequently felt that their own feelings of grief and loss were somehow inappropriate, and should not be acknowledged. The cultural expectation that pregnancy and childbirth are women's business, and that a man has no right to grieve for a wanted and imagined child, combined with strong sanctions against emotional expression among men, mean that the emotions of men in these circumstances are unlikely to be dealt with. Men, it seems, are less likely than women to blame themselves for the loss of a pregnancy (McGreal *et al.* 1997) but they are still likely to feel the loss.

A related phenomenon is the role of men in their partners' abortion decisions. While not all pregnant women have a partner to involve in the decision, those who do almost always discuss the decision with him (Resnick *et al.* 1994); men who are involved in such a decision generally take it extremely seriously (Coleman and Nelson 1998). Yet these issues are not ones on which psychological research has anything substantial to say.

These men's experiences epitomize the silence that surrounds men's relationships with fertility and with parenthood, and illustrate the need for research which brings the voices of men to greater prominence in areas traditionally regarded as only of relevance to women. This, in turn, might lead to models of fertility, infertility and parenthood that recognized the roles of cultural stereotypes and assumptions in individual subjectivities and that separated biological sex from culturally based gender.

Children with problems

Given hegemonic views of the father as a distant, emotionally uninvolved breadwinner, it is not surprising that psychological research on the family life of disabled or emotionally disturbed children has tended to focus on mothers and ignore fathers (Phares 1996, 1999). Where there are problems with children's physical and emotional health, it is assumed that this is the mother's, and not the father's, concern (Caplan and Hall-McCorquodale 1985; Phares 1992). The psychological literature overwhelmingly assumes that mothers are the main cause of their children's behavioural and emotional problems (Caplan and Hall-McCorquodale 1985; Phares 1992, 1996, 1999), and that mothers and not fathers will provide care when children's physical or emotional health requires it. This view simultaneously places unrealistic pressures on mothers, denies fathers' legitimate concerns for their children and promotes a rigidly gender-based view of 'appropriate' family roles which may bear no relation to the actual circumstances or preferences of individual families.

In this area, psychological research once again reflects and maintains a widespread cultural view that is frequently internalized by both men and women. A study of the families of intellectually disabled children (Heller *et al.* 1997) found that fathers spent less time providing care, experienced less caregiving burden, and were generally less affected by the child's problem, than mothers. On similar lines, Traustadottir (1991) found that fathers generally contributed to the caregiving of disabled children by providing financial support, by expressing appreciation of the mothers' work, and by discussing the child's care or treatment, but by contributing none of the actual work. This asymmetrical level of involvement was seen by both fathers and mothers as entirely appropriate, as much as could possibly be expected, and as showing profound depths of love and commitment on the part of the fathers.

Thus, fathers are defined out of involvement with their own children, regardless of the preferences they might have had. Although some health services do make some attempts to include fathers in the care of their disabled children (for example West 1998), this is still regarded as quite exceptional; fathers who choose to involve themselves in their children's care are viewed as atypical and it is assumed that most fathers will be uninterested in the day-to-day care of their children, unavailable most of the time, and less competent than their female partners at providing care.

As might be expected, fathers who do provide care for children with health problems appear to experience much the same burdens and satisfactions as mothers in the same circumstances. For example, Pruchno and Patrick (1999) surveyed men and women who had an adult child with a chronic disability, and found them to experience much the same stresses, and access much the same resources in order to cope.

Other aspects of family caregiving are also predominantly female, both in practice and in cultural construction (Lee 1999). Caring for frail, demented or chronically ill family members at home is predominantly female-typed, with surveys from several countries indicating that over 75 per cent of all family carers are women (Orbell 1996). Hooyman and Gonyea (1995: 3) have argued that 'men tend to assume primary responsibility of relatives with disabilities . . . only when a female family member is unavailable'.

Of course, men do take on the burden of family caregiving (Chang and White-Means 1991), just as they do the care of their own children, and there is evidence (for example Fisher 1994; Fuller-Jonap and Haley 1995) that these men experience the burdens and satisfactions of caring in a similar way to female caregivers. But when men do care for family members, this is still regarded at both a societal and a personal level as transgressive and inappropriate.

With growing numbers of men in same-sex relationships developing AIDS and related diseases, it has been argued that the extent to which men involve themselves in caregiving may increase (for example LeBlanc et al. 1995), but men with male partners have already transgressed hegemonic views of masculinity and thus they are not generally perceived as part of the social mainstream, not as men whose experiences should be seen as appropriate models for other men.

At an individual level, men are likely to internalize the view that they are essentially unable to provide care. Even men who cared full time for their disabled wives considered that their gender made them less able to carry out the role than women, feeling that women were naturally better caregivers than men, and that they had been forced by circumstance into an inappropriate and arduous role (Kaye and Applegate 1990). Providing intimate services such as washing and toileting in particular is seen as inappropriate for men, and demeaning both to the carer and the family member in a way which is not paralleled with female caregivers.

Male caregivers are more likely than female caregivers to receive help from outside the household (Stoller and Cutler 1992), suggesting a widespread view that men are less capable than women of fulfilling this role appropriately. Further, married women are more likely to receive formal care than are married men, while there is no difference for single people, again suggesting a gender difference in the perceived appropriateness of men and women providing care (Mutchler and Bullers 1994).

Kaye and Applegate (1990) have argued that there is a need for more targeted research on the experiences and needs of male caregivers, and on male styles of caring. The assumption that caregiving is 'naturally' women's work tends to render men's caregiving invisible, so that research in this area would need to be socially and theoretically critical and reflexive.

At a societal level, gender-based stereotypes about capacity to provide appropriate care to children and the dependent continue to shape social and economic policy (Hooyman and Gonyea 1995). Men are less likely than women to work in occupations which allow for part-time or other alternative working arrangements to accommodate the needs of family members. Female-dominated occupations, such as nursing and teaching, often have structural arrangements in place to allow workers to balance employment and family commitments, while male-dominated occupations generally do not. A feminist approach to family responsibility would be one in which genuine choices were available to family members, both male and female, regardless of their career choices, by providing social structures which allowed people who were willing to care for relatives in need to maintain paid work or otherwise to support themselves financially.

Divorce

Census data demonstrate that fathers are less likely to live in the same home as their children, compared to a generation ago; this trend is explained both by increases in divorce rates and by an increase in children born to unmarried women who do not maintain a relationship with the child's father (Long 1997). It is currently estimated that just under half of all first marriages will end in divorce, and the rate for second and subsequent marriages is even higher (for example Thompson and Amato 1999). In the majority of divorces and separations where small children are involved, children stay with their mothers, to the extent that the majority of psychological research on 'single-parent families' restricts itself entirely and uncritically to single-mother families (for example Saintonge et al. 1998; Clarke-Stewart et al. 2000). Although the terminology may be intended to be gender-inclusive, the use of the neutral term disguises an important asymmetry in parenting. Once again, parenthood is defined as women's business by default. Men who bring up their own children are ignored, with very few exceptions (for example Greif 1995). Men who want to continue to maintain a strong relationship with their own children face structural and systemic barriers (Pasley and Minton 1997; Baker and McMurray 1998). Long (1997) has argued that demographic changes have further confused the role of fathers, and tended to devalue their role, to the point that fathers are seen as optional in the upbringing of their children.

Research on the effects of divorce has, again, tended to ignore the impact on men and has focused on the impact on children. But the evidence does suggest that men find divorce difficult emotionally, more than do women. This is reflected most dramatically in suicide rates. Suicide rates among women are not affected by marital status (Cantor and Slater 1995; Kposowa 2000), although they are strongly influenced by motherhood status; people of either sex who take the main responsibility for the care of children have extremely low suicide rates (Appleby 1996). Men, on the other hand, have rates of suicide during and after marital separation which are between two and six times as high as those for married men (Cantor and Slater 1995; Kposowa 2000).

Divorce and separation are initiated by women more often than by men (Stevens and Gardner 1994) and thus men are less likely than women to be emotionally prepared for separation. Further, men's greater reluctance to engage in emotional expression (discussed in Chapter 3) may mean that divorce and family breakdown present difficulties which differ from those experienced by women, and negotiating satisfactory roles and relationships as non-custodial parents, stepfathers and single fathers is a challenge for which there are few successful role models (Pasley and Minton 1997).

Divorced men do experience worse physical health and have less healthy lifestyles than married men (Cheung 1998), but to a great degree these differences may be explained by pre-existing differences in variables such as alcohol use and aggressiveness, which tend to predispose men towards relationship breakdown. Emotionally, divorced men are more depressed than married men, although those who continue to live with their children or maintain close ties with them experience less severe depression (Shapiro and Lambert 1999). Depression among divorced parents has been demonstrated to affect levels of depression in adolescent offspring (Lorenz 1999), suggesting that fathers' distress may have longer-term repercussions on their families.

Most research that has examined men's lives after divorce has focused on the effects of men's lifestyles on their children. A meta-analysis (Amato and Gilbreth 1999) found that fathers' payment of child support was the strongest predictor of child well-being. This might seem to support the view that fathers' roles do revolve around financial support, and this effect may be a direct result of the child being able to live in material comfort, but an alternative explanation might be that payment of child support is an indicator that the father has an involved relationship with his children. With little effort made in most countries to enforce child support payments, the decision to follow a court order is to a large extent optional, and divorced men who support their children financially are often those who wish to maintain a fatherhood role. Children's well-being was also found to be associated with feelings of closeness between father and child and the quality of fathers' parenting, although not with the frequency of contact, again suggesting that fathers who maintain involvement and a warm relationship with their children will benefit those children as well as themselves.

The question of the effects of divorce and father absence on children's development is an open one. There is evidence to support the view that children whose fathers do not live with them show very much the same levels of intellectual and psychosocial development as children raised in other family circumstances (Hawkins and Eggebeen 1991), but other research suggests that children of divorce do show increases in behaviour problems (for example Morrison 1999). However, children's problems appear to be even greater if a marriage characterized by high levels of conflict does not break up (Morrison 1999); thus, fathers in conflictual relationships are in a situation of risking continuing harm to themselves and their children whatever decisions they make.

The nature of the father's continuing contact with his children, and his ability to develop a working relationship with his ex-partner, appear to be more influential in the well-being of children than the simple level of contact. While high levels of father contact might be expected to be unproblematically positive, King and Heard (1999) have shown that this is only the case when the mother is satisfied with the arrangements, and Lorenz (1999) has shown that girls in particular are affected by the level of continuing conflict between the parents. Differences in socialization mean that men are generally less skilled than women at the negotiation of relationships, and particularly tend to be less comfortable with explicit verbalization of emotions (Petersen 1998), a strategy which continues to form the basis of most relationship counselling. Thus, maintaining a civil relationship with one's children's other parent is a challenge for which men are often poorly prepared.

Conclusion

This chapter has illustrated the structural asymmetries in cultural expectations of men's and women's relationships with their families. Gender stereotypes which position men as primarily breadwinners, with neither interest nor ability in the practical aspects of family life, provide a disservice to both men and women, as well as to their children. Men face both internalized and structural barriers to close family involvement, and when relationships break down it seems that men find the transitions more difficult, and are more likely to lose contact with their children, than women.

Contemporary models of masculinity place incompatible demands on men. On the one hand, the traditional view of the distant husband and father, who supports his family financially but is otherwise uninvolved, is maintained by cultural discourses which simultaneously devalue the 'women's work' of childrearing and family caregiving, and position men as innately incapable of carrying out these tasks correctly. On the other hand, modern egalitarian attitudes to relationships between men and women demand that men take an equal share in childrearing and family life, despite systemic variables such as employment structures which make this ideal almost impossible to realize. Thus, men are caught in a dilemma, with every choice being less than ideal, and the fate of their relationships and the well-being of their children depending on their ability to negotiate their way through this social and personal minefield.

Summary

♦ Men's relationships with their families have not received the same attention by psychologists as have women's. This neglect appears to be grounded in an assumption that, for men, family roles are secondary and optional.
♦ Negotiating appropriate and satisfactory fatherhood roles places men in a structural dilemma. Men are enjoined to follow traditional and hegemonic models of fatherhood, maintaining a distant relationship with their children and contributing mainly in financial terms. At the same time, contemporary social discourses place value on an egalitarian approach to parenthood for both men and women. These conflicting social perspectives mean that any choice made by an individual man will, to a greater or lesser extent, transgress one or another social expectation.
♦ There is little evidence on men's roles in their families. What research does exist suggests that men who have close relationships with their children are emotionally healthier and have better relationships with their partners and children. Social expectations, structural forces and economic realities combine to make such a choice extremely difficult at an individual level.
♦ The fathers of children with physical and emotional problems are less likely than the mothers to be involved in their care, and social expectations militate against fathers' involvement in their children's difficulties.
♦ Men cope less well than women with divorce and relationship breakdown. Men who manage to maintain close relationships with their children after divorce benefit both themselves and their children, but again structural forces make this a difficult outcome to achieve.
♦ Expectations surrounding parenthood among men are also under-researched, but the little evidence does suggest that men, like women, grow up with the expectation that they will become parents, and are distressed by the unexpected inability to have children in much the same way as are women.

Additional reading

Hawkins, A.J. and Dollahite, D.C. (eds) (1997) *Generative Fathering: Beyond Deficit Perspectives*. Thousand Oaks, CA: Sage.
Lupton, D. and Barclay, L. (1997) *Constructing Fatherhood: Discourses and Experiences*. London: Sage.
Marsiglio, W. (ed.) (1995) *Fatherhood: Contemporary Theory, Research, and Social Policy*. Thousand Oaks, CA: Sage.

Men and ageing

Traditionally, psychological research on ageing has been conducted from a reductionist, biomedical model, assuming that illness, disability and emotional distress are inevitable consequences of the biological processes of ageing within the individual. It tends to focus on the problems associated with ageing rather than on the circumstances under which people may be described as 'ageing well', to ignore the social conditions and cultural stereotypes that may contribute to dysfunction and distress in older people, and to assume that gender is irrelevant in old age.

Negative stereotypes about ageing lead to stigmatization of older people and neglect of issues concerning them. Researchers, service providers and policy-makers frequently have an inaccurate understanding of old age, assuming that the majority of older people are frail, cognitively impaired, and uninterested in contemporary social issues; thus, services are often less than appropriate (Fennell et al. 1988). Older people are assumed to be a problem group and a burden on the community. The view that they may be successful survivors of life's vicissitudes, with a range of interesting experiences, potentially valuable insights, and coping strategies from which others can benefit, is not widespread, either in the research community or in society more generally (Wells and Freer 1988) and has until relatively recently been almost completely ignored in psychological research on ageing.

The extent of variation in health and well-being within an age cohort tends to increase with age. The young-old, up to around 70 or 75, frequently continue in good health and maintain active involvement with family and community, although as they age a growing minority does demonstrate increasing levels of disability. While the proportion in poor health or with significant disabilities certainly increases with age, the majority are not radically different from middle-aged adults in health, functioning and psychological well-being. It is the old-old (over 75) who have the highest probability of poor health and social isolation (Field and Minkler 1993) and gender differences in social functioning and behaviour begin to make a major contribution to well-being in this as in other age groups. The old-old, by definition, are people who have survived longer than most of their contemporaries and the concept of 'successful ageing' (Seeman 1994) becomes particularly relevant. While biological characteristics may in part be responsible for their continuing good health, the effects of a lifetime of gendered experience become increasingly important (for example Caspi and Elder 1986).

Research into ageing needs to balance a lifecourse perspective with an appreciation of cohort effects (Goldscheier 1990). Men who are in their eighties at the beginning of the twenty-first century, for example, will have grown up in a time of relatively inflexible gender roles and, while some will have adopted new perspectives as their broader social contexts have changed, many will take these attitudes and expectations into old age. Men in their sixties, by contrast, have grown up in a society which has seen enormous changes in gender relations, including the entry of the majority of women into the paid workforce, changes in expectations about marriage and parenthood, and a weakening of men's traditional family and social roles. Thus, they are likely to enter old age with different attitudes, and with different family structures and histories, than their fathers' generation. Men's expectations and life experiences are very different across generations, and one cannot assume that observed differences between men of different ages are a result of ageing, nor that each generation of men will age in the same way (Goldscheier 1990).

A lifecourse perspective on older men's health views their health and functioning as inextricably embedded in a lifetime of experiences. Lifecourse models of ageing which emphasize the effects of childhood and earlier adult experiences are essential in understanding how people come to have different degrees of functioning in old age (Ford and Sinclair 1987). While the lifecourse approach does acknowledge psychological, social and cultural influences on health, it has in general neglected the gendered nature of those influences.

The consideration of ageing from a gendered perspective is a relatively recent phenomenon (Thompson 1996). The majority of research in this area has arisen from an interaction of lifecourse perspectives on ageing with a feminist approach to scholarship, and has focused on women (for example Lewis 1985; Belgrave 1993; Gatz et al. 1995; Sharpe 1995). It is also the case that there are more older women than older men; 44 per cent of people aged 65 to 79 in Britain, for example, are men, and only 30 per cent of people aged 80 and over are men (Social Trends 1995). This in itself means that the experience of ageing is different for men and for women. While there is at least some feminist research on the typical experiences of older women, including widowhood, social isolation and the impact of social and family expectations of appropriate behaviour for older women (for example Byles *et al.* 1999; Feldman *et al.* 2001), the research literature is silent on the parallel experiences of older men. If women are more likely to be widowed, men are more likely to die and leave a partner. If older women increasingly become a majority in their age cohort, older men become a shrinking minority. How these facts influence individual men, and how they interact with gendered expectancies that men should dominate and control their social environment, has yet to be explored.

The argument that ageing is best viewed in the context of gendered life trajectories, including gender-based differences in physical health, financial and social resources, and life events, is as legitimate for men as it is for women (Barer 1994). In fact, Patterson *et al.* (1992) have demonstrated that negative circumstances earlier in the lifecourse, such as deprivation and poverty in childhood, appear to affect older men's physical and emotional health to a greater extent than they do women's. Similarly, Strawbridge *et al.* (1993), in a longitudinal study of older Americans, found that income, education and marital status were more important predictors of continued physical functioning in older age for men than for women. Even in Norway, with egalitarian and relatively generous state provision for older people, older men's previous socio-economic class continues to predict health, suggesting that the legacy of poverty in childhood or young adulthood is still felt at this age (Dahl and Birkelund 1997). On the other hand, the advantages of patriarchy for men mean that older men have, in general, experienced more advantageous financial and social conditions during their lifecourse and thus are more likely to reach old age in good health than are women (Smith and Baltes 1998). Research on the interactions between gendered life experiences and gendered life expectancies in older age could provide a framework for exploring the particular issues confronting men as they age, but such a research agenda does not as yet exist.

Research on ageing is also largely silent on the experiences of men and women whose lives have diverged from normative social expectations over the lifecourse. In particular, there is very little research on ageing among homosexual men. The concerns of older homosexual men have many overlaps with those of other older men and include anxiety, financial difficulties, bereavement and issues surrounding intimacy, loneliness and sexuality, but they are also affected by a history of homophobia and marginalization. Having dealt with these issues over a lifetime and having learned to be successfully homosexual in a heterosexual culture may have provided these and other marginalized people with skills and coping strategies which are advantageous in old age (McDougall 1993). Thus, their experiences not only are of interest in their own right but also may provide valuable insights into strategies for successful ageing for other men.

There is good evidence that gay men cope with the challenges of ageing at least as well as do heterosexual men (Kimmel 1993). This can be ascribed at least in part to these men being likely to have developed positive coping strategies over a lifetime of marginalization and stigmatization (McDougal

1993). Successful ageing and the development of positive coping skills is particularly characteristic of gay men who are highly satisfied with their gay identity (Adelman 1990), who identify publicly as gay, and who are active members of the gay community (Quam and Whitford 1992). In fact, Friend (1989) has suggested that older homosexual people who are prepared to challenge heterosexist social arrangements and assumptions are in fact likely to cope better with the challenges of ageing that other homosexual or heterosexual men.

Dorfman *et al.* (1995), surveying homosexual individuals aged between 60 and 93, found no support for the stereotype that older gay men are depressed, friendless and socially isolated. Compared to older heterosexual respondents, homosexual people receive more social support from friends and less from family, suggesting that health-care professionals need to be aware of the importance of non-family relationships among older gay men. Ehrenberg (1996), reviewing evidence on ageing and mental health among gay men and women, has pointed out that the research has tended to focus on relatively affluent and well-educated people. Although these people are generally shown to be in good psychological health and possessed of strong supportive social network, she points out that little is known of the ageing experiences of those with fewer economic, social and personal resources.

Ageing and health

While physical health does decline in old age, the rate at which this happens is extremely variable and is affected by a combination of genetic, behavioural, social and economic factors (Gatz *et al.* 1995). Chapter 2 has shown that women have a longer life expectancy, but that men tend to have lower levels of morbidity; this effect continues into old age. In an Australian study of over-seventies, Jorm *et al.* (1998) found that men were more likely than women of the same age to meet their criteria for 'successful ageing', which included living independently in the community, having positive self-rated health, and showing no indication of cognitive deficits.

The multidimensional and subjective nature of health and well-being is very much apparent among older people. The majority of older men (and women) rate their overall health as good, very good, or excellent even though most older people have at least one diagnosed chronic illness, such as diabetes, heart disease or arthritis (for example McCallum *et al.* 1994). Self-rated health is an excellent predictor of survival (for example McCallum *et al.* 1994). Although it is closely related to other variables such as major illnesses, disability, depression, and social support, it is also predicted by psychological variables such as life satisfaction (Rodin and McAvay 1992); there is research to suggest that it continues to predict survival among men even after controlling for demographic, socioeconomic, health status, and psychosocial factors (Wolinsky and Johnson 1992).

Physical health in old age is strongly affected by health-related behaviour in younger and middle age, but the maintenance of behaviours that are important in earlier life will continue to predict survival in later life. In a study of men aged between 65 and 74, Davis et al. (1994) showed that risk factors such as smoking, lack of physical activity, unhealthy use of alcohol, and obesity continued to predict mortality, casting doubt on widely held views that it is 'too late' for older people to adopt healthy lifestyles (Gabhainn et al. 1999). The promotion of healthy lifestyles among older men is a neglected area of research. There is some focus on under-nutrition, which is a particular problem for older people, especially widowers and others who live alone (Zipp and Holcomb 1992), but otherwise there is surprisingly little on positive strategies to maximize well-being in older age. Although there is evidence (for example Evans 1995) that physical activity can increase fitness, strength, health and functional capacity among older men, cultural stereotypes about appropriate activities for older people mean that exercise and other health-promoting activities do not receive the emphasis that they otherwise might.

Older adults generally accept some physical decline as normal and to be expected, and although they do regard poor health as a major disadvantage of ageing, many older people take a broad holistic view of health, and weigh up some loss of physical capacity against increases in free time and freedom of choice (Harris et al. 1989). Despite the reorientation of expectations and life goals which seems to accompany successful ageing, there remains for many a great fear of losing one's cognitive abilities (Freer 1988). The evidence suggests, though, that cognitive functioning remains normal for the majority of older people. While many people may become somewhat forgetful or show evidence of cognitive slowing, this does not interfere to any appreciable extent with their ability to live independently and maintain social relationships. A German study of the very old (Fichter et al. 1995) found that 21 per cent of men and women aged over 85 met clinical criteria for dementia, with the great majority showing normal cognitive functioning. A Dutch study of the same age group (Heeren et al. 1991) categorized 23 per cent as experiencing dementia, but just over half of these were categorized as 'mild', exhibiting slight losses in memory and concentration which did not interfere with independent living. While the prevalence increased with age, from 19 per cent among 85- to 89-year-olds to 32 per cent among 90- to 94-year-olds and 41 per cent aged 95 or over, most with any symptoms at all were classified as mildly demented, even in the oldest group. Jorm et al. (1987), integrating data from a number of surveys, concluded that clinical levels of dementia occurred among 2–3 per cent of those aged 65–74, 7–8 per cent of those aged 75–84 and 24 per cent of those aged 85 and over. In other words, even among the oldest, most people maintain normal cognitive functioning. The assumption and fear that old age inevitably means losing intellectual abilities is not justified.

Another popular misconception is that old age is inevitably associated with depression. However, there is good evidence that this is not the case; surveys in several countries find consistently low levels of depression among the old, although the differences between men and women are variable. Wells and Stacey (1998), for example, found very low rates of depression among Australians over 65, with the rate of depression among men being half that of women. In this study, the gender difference could be explained by differences in physical health, dependency for activities of daily living, and most importantly widowed status. In other words, older women were more likely to be depressed than older men, largely because they were more likely to be living alone and in poor health. On the other hand, a Finnish study of non-demented adults aged 85 and older (Paeivaerinta *et al.* 1999) found higher rates of depression among men than among women. Again, though, poor physical health was a strong predictor of depression; a Dutch study (Beekman *et al.* 1995) showed that the relationship between physical ill health and depression was stronger among older men than older women. Similarly, Lubben (1988) found that physical health and social networks were the best predictors of psychological well-being in a sample of older Americans.

These findings suggest that it is not age or gender *per se* which leads to depression; rather, the older that one is, the greater is the probability that one will experience poor health, pain and disability, and will lack social networks and support. Thus, social interventions which aim to prevent poverty, isolation and illness may go a long way in the prevention of psychological distress in older people, and may be particularly important for older men living alone, whose social networks tend to be smaller than those of women living alone (Arber and Ginn 1994).

Social relationships and well-being

The relationship between social connectedness and health is another area in which a gendered approach is needed. Informal social activity and the maintenance of friendships remain to a certain extent female-typed activities, and current generations of older people were socialized in a society in which men's and women's relationships with friends and family were expected to be different. Older women in general have better social resources than older men and seem better able to make new friends and cope positively with changed circumstances (Arber and Ginn 1994). Further, women's socialization throughout their lifetimes mean that they generally have better skills in developing and maintaining intimate friendships (Porcino 1985) which are increasingly valuable as social networks and opportunities for social interaction diminish with age. In Britain, 69 per cent of women aged over 75 live alone, compared with 35 per cent of men (Social Trends 1995). On the other hand, there is evidence that men cope better than women with smaller social networks (Shye *et al.* 1995) and level of social support is not as strongly predictive of survival among older men as among older women (Forster and Stoller 1992; Rennemark and Hagberg 1999). Financial circumstances, by contrast, seem to affect men more than women (de Leon *et al.* 1994).

For many men, social relationships and a sense of identity are inextricably intertwined with paid employment, and retirement is a major life event which symbolizes the transition from middle to later life. While most men have positive views of retirement, expecting an opportunity for new beginning, positive changes and more time for enjoyment (Gee and Baillie 1999), many men's work histories do not fit the stereotyped image of a long and stable career rewarded by a well-funded retirement (Hayward *et al.* 1998); retirement may be both financially and psychologically problematic for men who have not had what might be considered a normative career.

The relationships between retirement and health are complex and affected by gender, and again must be understood in the context of life experience (Moen 1996). Men's retirement decisions are less directly affected by life events and the health of other family members than are women's (Szinovacz and Washo 1992). Financial, health and work-related variables may act both positively and negatively both on men's retirement decisions and on their health. Quick and Moen (1998), in a small US survey, found that men were somewhat more satisfied with retirement than were women. The most satisfied men were those who had good physical health, and had enjoyed their pre-retirement job, planned their retirement, and retired at a time of their own choosing. Generally, those who have led comfortable adult lives are those who are most likely to make positive retirement transitions: unsurprisingly, men who experienced stability and security in their careers and retired with better pension benefits are likely to have better physical and emotional health in retirement (Hayward *et al.* 1998). Financial strain is a strong predictor of depression among older men (de Leon *et al.* 1994), more important for men than it is for women. Thus, while older men are actually less likely than older women to live in poverty (Gatz *et al.* 1995), men who lack financial resources seem to have more difficulties than women in similar circumstances.

It is worth noting that changes in the structure of employment, such an increased casualization of the workforce and fragmentation of men's work careers, mean that future generations of men are less likely to achieve these desirable retirement circumstances. Increasingly, men may be less able to support themselves and their dependent families financially in later life. Men may be forced by financial circumstances and by gendered expectations about men's responsibilities into longer working lives than they might ideally choose, with possible negative effects on health and well-being. Currently, men who choose to continue with paid employment into their seventies can be described as being in good health, committed to their jobs,

and negative about retirement; they are generally well-educated professionals, often have wives in employment, and have made a positive decision
to continue their working life (Parnes and Somers 1994). Subsequent generations of older men are likely to be quite different, with their retirement
decisions made under greater financial constraints. Thus, future cohorts of
men who continue to work into their seventies or beyond may have less
positive experiences.

Experiences of retirement are as heterogeneous as those associated with
any other major life event. Myers and Booth (1996) have demonstrated
that retirement is a major life change that tends to affect all aspects of the
individual's life and to impact on social relationships. The effect is positive
if the man leaves a high-stress job while it tends to be more negative if
he is in poor health at retirement, if his partner continues to work, and if
retirement is associated with reductions in social support. Although social
participation seems generally less important for men's health than it is for
women's, it is particularly important for life satisfaction among retired
men (Harlow and Cantor 1996).

The most important social relationship in most people's lives is that with
their marriage partner. The assumption that gender roles and sexual orientation become less important with age may be connected to the assumption
that older people are no longer sexually interested or active (Wetle 1991)
and the distaste with which younger people frequently regard sexuality
among elderly individuals (Slater 1995). There is little research which
addresses relationship quality among older men, or its impact on health and
well-being. What little that exists tends to focus, in a reductionist fashion,
on sexual behaviour and specifically on heterosexual penetrative sex. This
research seems to arise from a view that the only thing that matters about
a man's relationships is his heterosexual prowess. It is silent on the quality
or nature of older men's relationships with their partners, and has nothing
to say on the relationships of homosexual men, single men, divorced men,
and men who form new intimate relationships in later life.

A review of heterosexual men's sexuality and ageing (Schiavi 1990) demonstrated that there are significant age-related reductions in sexual desire,
arousal, activity and erectile capacity, but that most older men adjust to these
changes and their levels of sexual and marital satisfaction do not decrease.
Older people in long-term marriages generally have relationships which are
more positive and successful than those of younger people (Levenson et al.
1993), and for most older men, sexual activity comes to an end only with
their death or major disability, or that of their partner (Aiken 1989).

A national survey of married Americans (Marsiglio and Donnelly 1991)
found that 53 per cent of those over 60, including 23 per cent of those aged
over 75, reported that they were currently sexually active. Similar results
were obtained in a more recent study of men aged between 58 and 94
(Bortz et al. 1999); while erectile problems increased with age, most men
continued to be sexually active and to have a positive attitude to sexual

activity; their health status and their partner's interest in sex were the best predictors of continued sexual activity into old age.

There is little research on sexual activity among ageing homosexual men, possibly because of particularly negative stereotypes about ageing for homosexual men. A survey of 87 gay men aged between 40 and 77 (Pope and Schulz 1990) showed that 91 per cent of the respondents were still sexually active, that the majority reported no change in their level of interest in, or enjoyment of, sexual activity, and that there were few differences between middle-aged and older men.

Beyond this focus on the hydraulics of sex, research has largely ignored older men's intimate relationships. For both men and women, widowhood is one of the most important life events in older age. Because men have a shorter life expectancy than women and marry women who are, on average, a couple of years younger than them, men are less likely than women to be widowed. The Australian Bureau of Statistics (1995) estimates that only 20 per cent of Australian men will be widowed. Older men are also considerably more likely than older women to remarry (for example Wu 1995), with Schneider et al. (1996) finding that 61 per cent of men and 19 per cent of women had remarried within 25 months of widowhood. This difference is at least in part explained by the gender imbalance in older age groups, meaning that there are more opportunities for older widowed men than women to find appropriate partners.

Spousal bereavement can be expected to be a devastating loss, although reactions to the loss are highly individual and affected by the circumstances surrounding the death (Zisook and Shuchter 1991; Smith and Zick 1996). Certainly bereavement, whether of a spouse or another close family member, has consistent adverse effects on the well-being of older adults, both male and female (for example Arbuckle and de Vries 1995; Byrne and Raphael 1999); high levels of grief, depression and dysphoria are a normal reaction (for example Bruce et al. 1990). In the longer term, though, bereaved partners frequently demonstrate considerable resilience and coping ability. Within a little over a year most bereaved people report a sense that, although they continue to grieve and to miss their partner, they are starting to pick up their lives again and are adjusting as well as could be expected (Zisook and Shuchter 1991).

Although most research on bereavement does not consider the role of gender, loss of a spouse does seem to impact differently on women and on men, in ways that are also affected by culture, social circumstances, age at bereavement, and a range of other factors (Stroebe 1998; Wisocki and Skowron 2000). Particular issues arise for gay men, who are likely to face structural barriers in most health and legal systems, which do not recognize same-sex partners as legitimate spouses, but it is also the case that older gay men are likely to have developed additional coping strategies across their lifetimes, which may make them unexpectedly resilient (for example McDougall 1993).

Recently bereaved men are more likely than women to die from all causes (Clayton 1990), including suicide (for example Li 1995). Several researchers (for example Jacobs *et al.* 1989; Thompson *et al.* 1991; de Leon *et al.* 1994; Gilbar and Dagan 1995) have found that women experience more bereavement-related distress than men and have more difficulty adjusting to widowed life. On the other hand, others (for example Lee *et al.* 1998; van Grootheest *et al.* 1999) have found that men experienced more depression than women following widowhood. Lee *et al.* (1998) argued that this greater adjustment difficulty might be explained by the older age of widowed men, and by the fact that widowhood may in some senses be considered normative among older women. Older men may expect to die before their wives, may feel unprepared for widowhood, are less likely to know men who have been widowed, and will have fewer personal and social models for adjustment. Van Grootheest *et al.* (1999) explained men's greater difficulty by arguing that men may be less prepared than women to adapt to the changes in social support, and to the need to adjust their approach to finances and to housekeeping.

The relationship between social support and health among men is open to question, with research cited earlier suggesting that social support is less important to men than to women. However, the loss or lack of a partner is certainly associated with loneliness and negative affect. Some researchers (for example Peters and Liefbroer 1997; Thuen 1997) have actually found men to be more influenced by loss of social support following widowhood than are women, and widowed men to receive less social support than widowed women. On the other hand, Riggs (1997) found older widowed men to be more successful than expected in maintaining old friendships and forming new ones; this played an important role in their coping with bereavement.

Umberson *et al.* (1992) found that problems in coping with household management predicted depression among men following bereavement, while level of financial strain predicted depression following bereavement in women. This suggests that having to deal with other-gender-typed activities may be a source of difficulty for people who suddenly find themselves without a spouse. While this may be the case among the current generation of older people, subsequent generations who have grown up with less rigid assumptions about the gender appropriateness of particular activities may experience the adjustments differently. A similar argument may be raised with reference to the findings of Schut *et al.* (1997), who found that an emotion-focused counselling group was most useful for widowed men, while a problem-focused group was more useful for women, and concluded that people benefited most from learning about relatively unfamiliar and new coping strategies. It may be that later generations of older men feel less constrained by traditional gender roles and more able to adopt new coping strategies in order to deal with changed circumstances. The fact that widowed men are also more likely than women to adopt unhealthy eating patterns and abuse alcohol (for example Byrne *et al.* 1999) may also be a generational effect.

If men are less likely than women to be widowed, it is logically the case that men are more likely to die leaving a bereaved spouse. While there is a substantive psychological literature on dying and death, none of this takes an explicitly gendered perspective, none explores the experiences of men who must plan their lives in the expectation that they will die before their spouses. Conversely, there is little which deals with the expectation among women that they will be widowed. This lack may, once more, be based on the assumption that gender is irrelevant to people who are dying. While sexual activity may well cease during a terminal illness, this is not always the case (Jones 1988) and, even if it does, this does not mean that dying people are no longer gendered beings. Again, a lifetime of gendered experience will continue to impact on people's lives while they are dying.

Conclusion

Ageing is a time of life during which difficult challenges, including illness, disability, bereavement and approaching death, need to be dealt with. However, unremittingly negative social and professional attitudes to ageing make it even more difficult for older people to cope. The re-education of health professionals, together with an increase in the focus of research on understanding positive ageing (Seeman 1994), may be useful in the provision of appropriate services for older people and in the reduction of avoidance and rejection, so that people will prepare for old age in a more positive and optimistic way. A broader perspective on older people, as successful survivors of a lifetime of experience, and one that takes the gendered nature of that experience into account, is likely to benefit older men regardless of their personal life trajectories. A focus on the gendered nature of men's experiences throughout the lifecourse has been absent from psychological research on ageing, and there is the capacity for an enriched understanding of men's lives by taking this into account.

Summary

♦ Psychological research on ageing is characterized by a focus on the individual, and by an assumption that ageing is necessarily a time of decline and depression. It also fails to take a lifecourse perspective, and to consider the gendered nature of ageing.
♦ Men tend to be in better physical health than women in old age, although their life expectancy is shorter. Men's health appears to be more affected by economic conditions and less by social conditions than women's.

◆ Major depression and loss of cognitive functioning are relatively rare in older people, despite widespread social expectations.
◆ Men tend to have smaller social networks than women in old age, but seem less strongly affected by network size or the nature of those relationships.
◆ Retirement is a major life event for men, which has highly variable effects depending in part on the individual's work history, financial circumstances, attitudes to retirement and interests outside work.
◆ There is little evidence on intimate relationships and health in older people. There is research on changes in biological sexual functioning in ageing men, and there is some evidence on long-term marital relationships. Psychology is, however, silent on the experiences of older gay men, single men, or others who do not embody normative expectations for ageing men.
◆ Widowhood is a major life challenge which appears to be harder for men than for women, at least in part because men are less likely than women to be widowed and are likely to have fewer resources to cope on their own.
◆ There is a need for research which takes a positive view of ageing and which explores aspects of successful ageing, and for research which takes a gendered view and conceptualizes ageing from a lifecourse perspective.

Additional reading

Goldscheier, F.K. (1990) The aging of the gender revolution: what do we know and what do we need to know?, *Research on Aging*, 12: 531–45.
Smith, J. and Baltes, M.M. (1998) The role of gender in very old age: profiles of functioning and everyday life patterns, *Psychology and Aging*, 13: 676–95.
Stroebe, M.S. (1998) New directions in bereavement research: exploration of gender differences, *Palliative Medicine*, 12: 5–12.

The psychology of men's health: a gendered perspective

The psychology of men's health is in its infancy, but it has the potential to develop into a rich, dynamic and socially relevant research area with applications at all levels of intervention from clinical psychology to the development and assessment of equitable social policy. The thoughtful combination of quantitative and qualitative research, and the use of a range of theoretical and epistemological perspectives, has already led to the development of strong and dynamic streams of scholarship applied to men's health in other discipline areas (for example Connell 1995; Mac an Ghaill 1996). This book represents part of a similar development in psychology, that will over the next few years produce a psychology of men's health that views men in their social context, that understands their health as a complex, interactive and multiply determined phenomenon, and that recognizes the diversity of men's experiences.

One purpose of this book has been to present an argument for a particular perspective on men and their health: that of focusing on socially constructed concepts of gender and the impacts that these have on individual men's behavioural choices and thus on their health. This approach may be contrasted with a more traditional, reductionist and 'piecemeal' approach to men's health: the identification of specific, isolated topics to be investigated individually without attention to the social or cultural context. Diseases which occur only in men, such as prostate cancer, and those which – despite the evidence – are thought of as particularly male-typed, such as heart disease, have been identified as the central issues in understanding men's health (Fletcher 1997). However, such an approach derives from a specific perspective: one that focuses exclusively on the individual rather than his social context, that seeks to explain men's health at a biological level without taking any other level of explanation into account, and that has an emphasis on major illness and death, rather than on the well-being of men throughout their lives.

We have argued that the psychology of men's health, to an even greater extent than the field of men's health in general, needs to address men primarily as social and gendered beings. Illnesses and illness behaviour are of course important topics, but must be approached from an integrated perspective that places them, with other aspects of men's health, in the context of cultural assumptions about men and their behaviour.

The research reviewed in this book derives from a variety of scientific epistemologies. Some has followed the traditions of classical experimental psychology (for example Kring and Gordon 1998), experimental social psychology (for example Barrett *et al.* 1998), quantitative survey methods (for example Katz *et al.* 1998) or the epidemiological analysis of administrative data (for example Li and Ozanne-Smith 2000), all of which sit comfortably within the traditions of psychological science and related disciplines. Clinical outcome research (for example Schut *et al.* 1997), surveys of clinicians' attitudes (for example Garnets *et al.* 1991) and expert clinical reviews (for example Shannon and Woods 1991) form another legitimate source of information about men's health. To this range of research techniques must also be added the broad range of qualitative methods, which are of particular value in research fields in which the personal and the social interact (Chamberlain and Murray 1999).

Qualitative research methods aim to allow the voices of research participants to be heard, rather than imposing the worldview of the researcher on them. They are of particular value in areas which are ill defined or stigmatized. Researchers trained in an empiricist tradition may find it difficult to appreciate the value of qualitative methods, but the intelligent and appropriate use of alternative approaches has the potential to make psychology much more inclusive and socially relevant (Bohan 1992), by exploring diversity and context, or by dealing with issues which have been excluded from a traditional scientific approach. For example, Smith's (1998) analysis of semi-structured interviews with full-time 'househusbands' and Lupton and Barclay's (1997) series of interviews with new fathers enabled a range of men to describe individual experiences that were both diverse and idiosyncratic, in a way that traditional quantitative research could not.

Several writers in women's health (Chesney and Ozer 1995; Stanton and Gallant 1995) have pointed to the need for a thoughtful combination of qualitative and quantitative methods, and a selection of methods on the basis of what will most appropriately address the research question. There are many questions in men's health research for which either qualitative or quantitative methods, or a combination of both, would be appropriate, and it is important to appreciate the different biases and thus the different outcomes that will arise from these different approaches. For example, Baxter and Bittman (1995) used quantitative time-use surveys to demonstrate that men spend less time than women in housework, regardless of their other roles. Quantitative research such as this can demonstrate the existence of a gender difference, but cannot consider the full range of possible reasons for this difference. Qualitative, unstructured interview work that invites men to explore the role of housework in their lives (for example Smith 1998), by contrast, says nothing directly about the usual gender distribution of this labour but does provide information on its stigmatized and stigmatizing nature for men. A consideration of both sets of results leads to a better, more comprehensive picture of the situation of domestic labour in men's lives and is likely to produce recommendations or outcomes that are congruent with the needs and perspectives of men themselves.

This book has attempted to set an agenda for research into the psychology of men's health which differs in three main ways from traditional health psychology. First, research should focus on health and well-being in its widest sense, rather than on illness. Second, it should emphasize the extent to which individual behavioural choices are constrained by the material, social, cultural and political context. Third, it should recognize and explore diversity among individuals and among groups of men. A psychology of men's health which has these three characteristics will also have as its final aim the promotion of social change and the development of strategies that will produce a more equitable society for both men and women.

Focus on health

Health psychology in general has been criticized for its overemphasis on illness, and its lack of attention to well-being and good physical health, and to the relationship between individual good health and social context (for example Marks 1996). A focus on illness or on specifically illness-related behaviours is consistent with the empiricist and reductionist epistemology of traditional psychology, but fails to consider health in its broadest context.

The major causes of death and ill health among men, heart disease and cancer, are also the primary causes of death among women (Australian Bureau of Statistics 2000); risk factors such as cigarette smoking, obesity and sedentary lifestyles are also similarly risky for both men and women. A gendered approach to men's health focuses, not on these specific behaviours and disease endpoints, but on the influences on, and determinants of, these behaviours: the social constructions which influence individual men's behavioural choices and thus affect their health behaviours and outcomes. Why, for example, are men more likely than women to exercise (Dubbert and Martin 1988), but less likely to adopt and maintain a healthy diet (Katz *et al.* 1998)? Strategies to improve men's health can be developed only if these gendered differences in behavioural choices are taken seriously, and the underlying differences in men's and women's social worlds adequately explored.

Men's health is more than physical functioning and more than the absence of illness. Health encompasses an individual's physiological state, psychological well-being and social context. This includes normal physiological processes such as growth and ageing; it includes the relationships between men and their families; it includes men's interactions with the wider society; and it includes both positive and negative aspects of cultural notions of masculinity, including violence and homophobia on the one hand, and the benefits to men of a male-oriented society on the other.

It is frequently pointed out that research on illness and its treatment has traditionally been conducted with male subjects, and the claim has been made that there is therefore no need for any additional focus on men's health. This well-established bias in biomedical research has been identified as disadvantageous to women (for example Rodin and Ickovics 1990; Stanton 1995). But it is also the case that traditional illness research has neglected the level of diversity that exists among men. A reductionist focus on the biological aspects of disease means that researchers tend to assume that differences between men from different cultural and ethnic backgrounds, of different ages, and with different lifestyles, must be irrelevant. Well-established evidence about the relationships between social circumstances and biological functioning thus tends to be ignored.

For example, it is well established that African American men are more prone to hypertension than are White American men (Pickering 1999). It has been further demonstrated that the darker a man's skin, the higher his risk both of hypertension and of racist experiences (Klonoff and Landrine 2000). This would suggest that the understanding and treatment of hypertension could benefit from the exploration of social inequalities, yet the majority of research on hypertension focuses on the individual rather than the context. Similar arguments can be raised for a wide range of illnesses and conditions that are traditionally thought of as essentially biological.

Research on illness and specific risk factors, therefore, does need to be expanded in order to take into account men's diverse social situations, and the stresses experienced by particular groups. Health psychology, however, needs to expand its perspective beyond illness and into issues for men's health throughout their lives. It is for this reason that this book has focused on men in the contexts of their families and societies: men as fathers and husbands, men as workers, men as individuals whose life choices are made in specific and gendered contexts.

Focus on context

Men's behaviours and their health are affected in obvious ways by social and cultural structures, systems and expectations. They can also be shown to be affected by systemic changes in employment and in family structure. This book has attempted to demonstrate that men are also affected more subtly by a sexist and heterosexist society, and by the myths and stereotypes promoted by hegemonic and prescriptive notions of masculinity. Men's choices are further constrained by a social context that values them for their economic productivity rather than for their ability to sustain positive relationships. The interactions between this context and any individual man's choices or behaviours regarding his health are complex, but must be understood if the psychology of men's health is to reflect this reality.

Research that focuses on individual behaviours such as attendance for screening or adopting healthy dietary patterns misses a fundamental point, which is that men's health is not a series of isolated problems which can, one by one, be understood and then subtracted from men's lives, until they have no health problems left. Men's health is better understood as arising from choices made within a complex interacting pattern of beneficial and damaging experiences, opportunities and expectations that can be understood only in their social, cultural and political context.

Psychology's tendency to emphasize the personal and to focus on subjective intra-individual causes of distress (Fox and Prilleltensky 1997), when applied to those whose lives are constrained by socio-economic circumstances or by prejudice, can lead to an implicit blaming of those people for their problems (Lee 1998b; Stanton and Gallant 1995). Thus, men who are unable to find paid work because of changes at a macro-economic level, or men whose sexual preferences are not those of the mainstream, are stigmatized and blamed for the problems they experience. An approach that considers the contexts of these men's lives may result in a more balanced perspective and ultimately produce strategies for intervention that are more helpful.

Focus on cultural sensitivity and diversity

An inclusive approach and the use of participants from diverse cultural, ethnic and racial backgrounds is another essential aspect of a contextualist approach to research into men's health. Cultural context and social conditions have tended to be marginalized in psychologists' explanations of behaviour (Jahoda 1988). Psychological textbooks and journals frequently give the impression that research has been carried out in a cultural vacuum. An individual-centred approach to both data and theory leads to an implicit assumption that 'the particular historical period or sociocultural context in which data have been collected is . . . of little or no importance' (Spence 1985: 1285). Most psychological theories of behaviour, attitude or choice are presented as if they had universal applicability. While race, nationality, age or sexual orientation may be acknowledged to affect minor details, they are generally viewed as having no impact on the 'real' relationships between 'important' variables.

For example, a wealth of research into possible biological determinants for the higher prevalence of violent behaviour in men than women takes on a new perspective when such behaviour is compared across different cultures, ranging from the Brazilian Yanomamo, for whom violence is almost an everyday occurrence, to the Hopi of North America whose spiritual injunctions against violence meant that such behaviour was almost unknown, even against oneself (Owens and Ashcroft 1985). Cross-cultural comparisons such as these make it clear that essentialist explanations of observed differences between men and women – explanations that rely on the notion that men 'just are' the way they are because of essential and unmodifiable differences from women – are simplistic and of limited use.

Psychology frequently assumes that minorities, including ethnic, religious or racial minorities, gay men, and people with disabilities or special needs, are basically the same as the White, middle-class, heterosexual men who are implicitly regarded as 'standard' human beings, and that their needs can be accommodated through minor modifications of existing theories, models and intervention strategies. Traditional science is embedded in a cultural discourse which describes some human attributes as normal and natural, and others as anomalous and in need of explanation. The 'normal human being' is implicitly assumed to be a heterosexual, middle-class, employed, able-bodied man. Where others differ from the 'norm', they are positioned as inevitably problematic and in need of investigation and correction (Harding 1986). A psychology of men's health can usefully recognize and challenge the arbitrary and prescriptive nature of these assumptions, and begin to develop models of men's behaviours in a range of social contexts, in order to understand the diversity of men's experiences.

Conclusion

Research and scholarship in the area of the psychology of men's health has been very limited but is a field with an exciting future. To a large extent, research on men's health has either taken a biomedical perspective on health and illness, or has made the assumption that 'normal' gender roles and differences, as defined in the particular time and place occupied by the researcher, are natural and immutable and thus do not need explication or critical evaluation.

Gender-based research in the psychology of men's health needs to move beyond the traditional individualism and subjectivism of psychological theory, and take sociocultural issues into account. Men's lives need to be examined in context, with an awareness of the diversity of men's experiences, and through a combination of both quantitative and qualitative research strategies. An awareness of the political nature of psychological research, of the implications inherent in apparently neutral decisions about what phenomena should be studied in what ways, is necessary to develop a truly inclusive and socially relevant psychology of men's health.

Summary

♦ The psychology of men's health, if it is to address issues of concern for contemporary men, needs to take account of the gendered social context within which men make individual health-related choices.
♦ This book argues that the psychology of men's health can usefully employ a range of research methods, from traditional reductionist, experimental and quantitative methods to qualitative strategies that enable men's experiences to be explored in context.
♦ The psychology of men's health needs to move beyond an exclusive focus on illnesses and illness behaviours to a broad social view of health that encompasses the study of men's health and well-being in its widest sense.
♦ The importance of studying men's health in context is particularly of relevance to studying the health behaviours of men who are marginalized or stigmatized.

An awareness of cultural diversity is an essential aspect of a gendered and socially relevant psychology of men's health that can contribute to a more equitable society.

References

Abell, S.C. and Richards, M.H. (1996) The relationship between body shape satisfaction and self-esteem: an investigation of gender and class differences, *Journal of Youth and Adolescence*, 25: 691–703.

Adams, S., Kuebli, J., Boyle, P.A. and Fivush, R. (1995) Gender differences in parent–child conversations about past emotions: a longitudinal investigation, *Sex Roles*, 33: 309–23.

Adelman, M. (1990) Stigma, gay lifestyles, and adjustment to aging: a study of later-life gay men and lesbians, *Journal of Homosexuality*, 20: 7–32.

Aiken, L.R. (1989) *Later Life*. Hillsdale, NJ: Lawrence Erlbaum.

Albarracin, D., Johnson, B.T., Fishbein, M. and Muellerleile, P.A. (2001) Theories of reasoned action and planned behavior as models of condom use: a meta-analysis, *Psychological Bulletin*, 127: 142–61.

Allen, S.M. and Hawkins, A.J. (1999) Maternal gatekeeping: mothers' beliefs and behaviors that inhibit greater father involvement in family work, *Journal of Marriage and the Family*, 61: 199–212.

Amato, P.R. and Gilbreth, J.G. (1999) Nonresident fathers and children's well-being: a meta-analysis, *Journal of Marriage and the Family*, 61: 557–73.

American Cancer Society (1994) *Cancer Facts and Figures, 1994*. Atlanta, GA: American Cancer Society.

Anderson, P., Bhatia, K. and Cunningham, J. (1996) *Mortality of Indigenous Australians*. (cat no. 3315.0). Canberra: Australian Bureau of Statistics.

Anonymous (1999) Atlas of injuries in the United States Armed Forces, *Military Medicine*, 164(8 suppl.).

Appleby, L. (1996) Suicidal behaviour in childbearing women, *International Review of Psychiatry*, 8: 107–15.

Apter, T. (1993) *Professional Progress: Why Women Still Don't Have Wives*. London: Macmillan.

Arber, S. and Ginn, J. (1994) Women and aging, *Reviews in Clinical Gerontology*, 4: 349–58.

Arbuckle, N.W. and de Vries, B. (1995) The long-term effects of later life spousal and parental bereavement on personal functioning, *Gerontologist*, 35: 637–47.

Archer, J., Birring, S.S. and Wu, F.C.W. (1998) The association between testosterone and aggression in young men: empirical findings and a meta-analysis, *Aggressive Behavior*, 24: 411–20.

Australian Bureau of Statistics (ABS) (1995) *Australian Women's Yearbook 1995*. Canberra: ABS.

Australian Bureau of Statistics (1996a) *Causes of Death 1994*. Canberra: ABS.

Australian Bureau of Statistics (1996b) *Prisoners in Australia, 1994*. Canberra: ABS.

Australian Bureau of Statistics (2000) *Deaths, Australia 1999* (cat no. 3302.0). Canberra: ABS.

Badinter, E. (1981) *The Myth of Motherhood: An Historical Overview of the Maternal Instinct*. London: Souvenir.

Bailey, J.R. and Eastman, W.N. (1994) Positivism and the promise of the social sciences, *Theory and Psychology*, 4: 505–24.

Bailey, W.T. (1994) A longitudinal study of fathers' involvement with young children: infancy to age 5 years, *Journal of Genetic Psychology*, 155: 331–9.

Baker, R. and McMurray, A.M. (1998) Contact fathers' loss of school involvement, *Journal of Family Studies*, 4: 201–14.

Ballard, C.G., Davis, R., Cullen, P.C., Mohan, R.N. and Dean, C. (1994) Prevalence of postnatal psychiatric morbidity in mothers and fathers, *British Journal of Psychiatry*, 164: 782–8.

Barer, B.M. (1994) Men and women aging differently, *International Journal of Aging and Human Development*, 38: 29–40.

Barnett, R.C. and Baruch, G.K. (1987) Determinants of fathers' participation in family work, *Journal of Marriage and the Family*, 49: 29–40.

Barrett, L.F., Robin, L., Pietromonaco, P. and Eyssel, K.M. (1998) Are women the more emotional sex? Evidence from emotional experiences in a social context, *Cognition and Emotion*, 12: 555–78.

Barry, H. and Schlegel, A. (1984) Measurement of adolescent sexual behaviour in the Standard Sample of Societies, *Ethnology*, 23: 315–29.

Barry, H. and Schlegel, A. (1985) Cultural customs that influence sexual freedom in adolescence, *Ethnology*, 24: 151–62.

Baruch, G.K. and Barnett, R. (1986) Role quality, multiple role involvement, and psychological well-being in midlife women, *Journal of Personality and Social Psychology*, 51: 578–85.

Baxter, J. (1997) Gender equality and participation in housework: a cross-national perspective, *Journal of Comparative Family Studies*, 28: 220–47.

Baxter, J. and Bittman, M. (1995) Measuring time spent on housework: a comparison of two approaches, *Australian Journal of Social Research*, 1: 21–46.

Baxter, J., Gibson, D. and Lynch-Blosse, M. (1991) *Doubletake: The Links between Paid and Unpaid Work*. Canberra: Australian Government Publishing Service.

Beekman, A.T.F., Kriegsman, D.M.W., Deeg, D.J.H. and van Tilburg, W. (1995) The association of physical health and depressive symptoms in the older population: age and sex differences, *Social Psychiatry and Psychiatric Epidemiology*, 30: 32–8.

Belgrave, L.L. (1993) Discrimination against older women in health care, in J.D. Garner and A.A. Young (eds) *Women and Healthy Aging: Living Productively in Spite of it All*. New York: Haworth.

Bell, N.S., Amoroso, P.J., Yore, M.M. *et al.* (2000) Self-reported risk-taking behaviors and hospitalization for motor vehicle injury among active duty Army personnel, *American Journal of Preventive Medicine*, 18(suppl. 3): 85–95.

Belsky, J. and Pensky, E. (1988) Marital change across the transition to parenthood, *Marriage and Family Review*, 12: 133–56.

Benazon, N., Wright, J. and Sabourin, S. (1992) Stress, sexual satisfaction, and marital adjustment in infertile couples, *Journal of Sex and Marital Therapy*, 18: 273–84.

Biglan, A., Glasgow, R.E. and Singer, G. (1990) The need for a science of larger social units: a contextual approach, *Behavior Therapy*, 21: 195–215.

Bird, C.E. (1999) Gender, household labor, and psychological distress: the impact of the amount and division of housework, *Journal of Health and Social Behavior*, 40: 32–45.

Bittman, M. (1992) *Juggling Time: How Australian Families Use their Time*. Canberra: Australian Government Publishing Service.

Bittman, M. and Lovejoy, F. (1993) Domestic power: negotiating an unequal division of labour within a framework of equality, *Australian and New Zealand Journal of Sociology*, 29: 302–21.

Blackwood, E. (2000) Culture and women's sexualities, *Journal of Social Issues*, 56: 223–38.

Blair, S.L. (1992) The sex-typing of children's household labor: parental influence on daughters' and sons' housework, *Youth and Society*, 24: 178–203.

Blair, S.L. and Lichter, D.T. (1991) Measuring the division of household labor: gender segregation of housework among American couples, *Journal of Family Issues*, 12: 91–113.

Blouin, A.G. and Goldfield, G.S. (1995) Body image and steroid use in male body builders, *International Journal of Eating Disorders*, 18: 159–65.

Bohan, J.S. (1992) Prologue: re-viewing psychology, re-playing women – an end searching for a means, in J.S. Bohan (ed.) *Seldom Seen, Rarely Heard: Women's Place in Psychology*. Boulder, CO: Westview.

Bolding, G., Sherr, L., Maguire, M. *et al.* (1999) HIV risk behaviours among gay men who use anabolic steroids, *Addiction*, 94: 1829–35.

Bortz, W.M., Wallace, D.H. and Wiley, D. (1999) Sexual function in 1,202 aging males: differentiating aspects, *Journals of Gerontology Series A, Biological Sciences and Medical Sciences*, 54A: M237–41.

Bostwick, T.D. and DeLucia, J.L. (1992) Effects of gender and specific dating behaviors on perceptions of sex willingness and date rape, *Journal of Social and Clinical Psychology*, 11: 14–25.

Bowlby, J. (1951) *Maternal Care and Mental Health*. Geneva: World Health Organization.

Bowles, S.V., James, L.C., Solursh, D.S. *et al.* (2000) Acute and post-traumatic stress disorder after spontaneous abortion, *American Family Physician*, 61: 1689–96.

Bridges, J.S. (1991) Perceptions of date and stranger rape: a difference in sex role expectations and rape-supportive beliefs, *Sex Roles*, 24: 291–307.

Brod, H. (ed.) (1987) *The Making of Masculinities: The New Men's Studies*. Boston, MA: Allen & Unwin.

Brod, H. and Kaufman, M. (eds) (1994) *Theorizing Masculinities*. London: Sage.

Brody, L.R. (1997) Gender and emotion: beyond stereotypes, *Journal of Social Issues*, 53: 369–93.

Brody, L.R. (1999) *Gender, Emotion, and the Family*. Cambridge, MA: Harvard University Press.

Broude, G.J. and Greene, S.J. (1976) Cross-cultural codes on twenty sexual attitudes and practices, *Ethnology*, 15: 409–29.

Brownell, K.D. (1991) Dieting and the search for the perfect body: where physiology and culture collide, *Behavior Therapy*, 22: 1–12.

Brownmiller, S. (1975) *Against our Will*. New York: Simon & Schuster.

Bruce, M.L., Kim, K., Leaf, P.J. and Jacobs, S. (1990) Depressive episodes and dysphoria resulting from conjugal bereavement in a prospective community sample, *American Journal of Psychiatry*, 147: 608–11.

Buckley, P., Freyne, A. and Walsh, N. (1991) Anorexia nervosa in males, *Irish Journal of Psychological Medicine*, 8: 15–18.

Bugge, I., Hendel, D.D. and Moen, R. (1985) Client evaluations of therapeutic processes and outcomes in a university mental health center, *Journal of American College Health*, 33: 141–6.

Buntaine, R.L. and Costenbader, V.K. (1997) Self-reported differences in the experience and expression of anger between girls and boys, *Sex Roles*, 36: 625–37.

Burman, E., Bewlay, C., Goldberg, B. *et al.* (eds) (1996) *Challenging Women: Psychology's Exclusions, Feminist Possibilities*. Buckingham: Open University Press.

Burr, J.A., McCall, P.L. and Powell-Griner, E. (1997) Female labor force participation and suicide, *Social Science and Medicine*, 44: 1847–59.

Buss, A.H. and Perry, M. (1992) The Aggression Questionnaire, *Journal of Personality and Social Psychology*, 63: 452–9.

Buss, D.M. (2000) *The Dangerous Passion: Why Jealousy is as Necessary as Love and Sex*. New York: Free Press.

Buss, D.M., Larsen, R.J., Westen, D. and Semmelroth, J. (1992) Sex differences in jealousy: evolution, physiology, and psychology, *Psychological Science*, 3: 251–5.

Byles, J.E., Feldman, S. and Mishra, G. (1999) For richer for poorer, in sickness and in health: older widowed women's health, relationships and financial security, *Women and Health*, 29: 15–30.

Byrne, G.J.A. and Raphael, B. (1999) Depressive symptoms and depressive episodes in recently widowed older men, *International Psychogeriatrics*, 11: 67–74.

Byrne, G.J.A., Raphael, B. and Arnold, E. (1999) Alcohol consumption and psychological distress in recently widowed older men, *Australian and New Zealand Journal of Psychiatry*, 33: 740–7.

Cameron, R., Redman, S., Burrow, S. and Young, B. (1995) Comparison of career patterns of male and female graduates of one Australian medical school, *Teaching and Learning in Medicine*, 7: 218–24.

Canetto, S.S. (1997) Meanings of gender and suicidal behavior during adolescence, *Suicide and Life-Threatening Behavior*, 27: 339–51.

Cantor, C.H. and Slater, P.J. (1995) Marital breakdown, parenthood, and suicide, *Journal of Family Studies*, 1: 91–102.

Caplan, P.J. and Caplan, J.B. (1999) *Thinking Critically about Research on Sex and Gender*. New York: Longman.

Caplan, P.J. and Hall-McCorquodale, I. (1985) The scapegoating of mothers: a call for change, *American Journal of Orthopsychiatry*, 55: 610–13.

Carach, C. and James, M. (1998) Homicide between intimate partners in Australia, *Trends and Issues (Australian Institute of Criminology)*, 90.

Caradoc-Davies, T. and Hawker, A. (1997) The true rates of injury among workers in New Zealand: comparing 1986 and 1991, *Disability and Rehabilitation*, 19: 285–92.

Carballo-Dieguez, A., Remien, R.H., Dolezal, C. and Wagner, G. (1997) Unsafe sex in the primary relationships of Puerto Rican men who have sex with men, *AIDS and Behavior*, 1: 9–17.

Carlat, D.J. and Camargo, C.A. (1991) Review of bulimia nervosa in males, *American Journal of Psychiatry*, 148: 831–43.

Carrigan, T., Connell, R. and Lee, J. (1985) Toward a new sociology of masculinity, *Theory and Society*, 14: 551–604.

Caspi, A. and Elder, G.H. (1986) Life satisfaction in old age: linking social psychology and history, *Psychology and Aging*, 1: 18–26.

Caverhill, P.A. (1997) Bereaved men: how therapists can help, *Psychotherapy in Private Practice*, 16: 1–16.

Chamberlain, K. and Murray, M. (1999) *Qualitative Health Psychology*. London: Sage.

Chan, D.K.S. and Cheung, S.F. (1998) An examination of premarital sexual behavior among college students in Hong Kong, *Psychology and Health*, 13: 805–21.

Chang, C.F. and White-Means, S.I. (1991) The men who care: an analysis of male primary caregivers who care for frail elderly at home, *Journal of Applied Gerontology*, 10: 343–58.

Chesney, M.A. and Ozer, E.M. (1995) Women and health: in search of a paradigm, *Women's Health: Research on Gender, Behavior, and Policy*, 1: 3–26.

Cheung, Y.B. (1998) Can marital selection explain the differences in health between married and divorced people? From a longitudinal study of a British birth cohort, *Public Health*, 112: 113–17.

Clark, J.M. (1995) Profeminist men's studies and gay ethics, *Journal of Men's Studies*, 3: 241–55.

Clarke-Stewart, K.A., Vandell, D.L., McCartney, K., et al. (2000) Effects of parental separation and divorce on very young children, *Journal of Family Psychology*, 14: 304–26.

Clayton, P.J. (1990) Bereavement and depression, *Journal of Clinical Psychiatry*, 51(suppl.): 34–8.

Coleman, P.K. and Nelson, E.S. (1998) The quality of abortion decisions and college students' reports of post-abortion emotional sequelae and abortion attitudes, *Journal of Social and Clinical Psychology*, 17: 425–42.

Collins, K.A. and Nichols, C.A. (1999) A decade of pediatric homicide: a retrospective study at the Medical University of South Carolina, *American Journal of Forensic Medicine and Pathology*, 20: 169–72.

Coltrane, S. (1982) The micropolitics of gender in nonindustrial societies, *Gender and Society*, 6(1): 86–107.

Coltrane, S. (1989) Household labour and the routine production of gender, *Social Problems*, 36: 473–90.

Coltrane, S. (1990) Birth timing and the division of labor in dual-earner families: exploratory findings and suggestions for future research, *Journal of Family Issues*, 11: 157–81.

Coltrane, S. (1995) The future of fatherhood: social, demographic, and economic influences on men's family involvements, in W. Marsiglio (ed.) *Fatherhood: Contemporary Theory, Research, and Social Policy*. Thousand Oaks, CA: Sage.

Coltrane, S. and Adams, M. (1997) Work–family imagery and gender stereotypes: television and the reproduction of difference, *Journal of Vocational Behavior*, 50: 323–47.

Coltrane, S. and Allan, K. (1994) 'New' fathers and old stereotypes: representations of masculinity in 1980s television advertising, *Masculinities*, 2: 43–66.

Connell, R.W. (1995) *Masculinities*. Sydney: Allen & Unwin.

Connell, R.W. (1998) Masculinities and globalization, *Men and Masculinities*, 1: 3–23.

Connolly, K.J., Edelmann, R.J., Cooke, I.D. and Robson, J. (1992) The impact of infertility on psychological functioning, *Journal of Psychosomatic Research*, 36: 459–68.

Cooney, T.M., Pedersen, F.A., Indelicato, S. *et al.* (1993) Timing of fatherhood: is 'on-time' optimal?, *Journal of Marriage and the Family*, 55: 205–15.

Cooper, C., Eslinger, D., Nash, D., al Zawahri, J., and Stolley, P. (2000) Repeat victims of violence: report of a large concurrent case-control study, *Archives of Surgery*, 135: 837–43.

Copenhaver, M.M. and Eisler, R.M. (1996) Masculine gender role stress: a perspective on men's health, in P. Kato and T. Mann (eds) *Handbook of Diversity Issues in Health Psychology*. New York: Plenum.

Cott, N. (1977) *The Bonds of Womanhood: Women's Sphere in New England, 1780–1835*. New Haven, CT: Yale University Press.

Courtenay, W.H. (1998) College men's health: an overview and a call to action, *Journal of American College Health*, 46: 279–90.

Courtenay, W.H. (2000) Engendering health: a social constructionist examination of men's health beliefs and behaviors, *Psychology of Men and Masculinity*, 1: 4–15.

Cubbins, L.A. and Tanfer, K. (2000) The influence of gender on sex: a study of men's and women's self-reported high-risk sex behavior, *Archives of Sexual Behavior*, 29: 229–57.

Cusick, L. and Rhodes, T. (2000) Sustaining sexual safety in relationships: HIV positive people and their sexual partners, *Culture, Health and Sexuality*, 2: 473–87.

Dahl, E. and Birkelund, G.E. (1997) Health inequalities in later life in a social democratic welfare state, *Social Science and Medicine*, 44: 871–81.

Daniluk, J.C. (1991) Strategies for counseling infertile couples, *Journal of Counseling and Development*, 69: 317–20.

Danseco, E.R., Miller, T.R. and Spicer, R.S. (2000) Incidence and costs of 1987–1994 childhood injuries: demographic breakdowns, *Pediatrics*, 105(2): E27.

Davis, C. and Katzman, M. (1997) Charting new territory: body esteem, weight satisfaction, depression, and self-esteem among Chinese males and females in Hong Kong, *Sex Roles*, 36: 449–59.

Davis, C. and Katzman, M. (1998) Chinese men and women in the United States and Hong Kong: body and self-esteem ratings as a prelude to dieting and exercise, *International Journal of Eating Disorders*, 23: 99–102.

Davis, D.L. (1993) When men become 'women': gender antagonism and the changing sexual geography of work in Newfoundland, *Sex Roles*, 29: 457–75.

Davis, M.A., Neuhaus, J.M., Moritz, D.J. and Segal, M.R. (1994) Health behaviors and survival among middle-aged and older men and women in the NHANES I Epidemiologic Follow-up Study, *Preventive Medicine*, 23: 369–76.

Davis, M.C., Matthews, K.A. and Twamley, E.W. (1999) Is life more difficult on Mars or Venus? A meta-analytic review of sex differences in major and minor life events, *Annals of Behavioral Medicine*, 21: 83–97.

Davis, T. and Lee, C. (1996) Sexual assault: myths and stereotypes among Australian adolescents, *Sex Roles*, 34: 787–803.

DeFrain, J., Martens, L., Stork, J. and Stork, W. (1990) The psychological effects of a stillbirth on surviving family members, *Omega – Journal of Death and Dying*, 22: 81–108.

DeFrain, J., Millspaugh, E. and Xie, X. (1996) The psychosocial effects of miscarriage: implications for health, *Family Systems Medicine*, 14: 331–47.

de Leon, C.F.M., Rapp, S.S. and Kasl, S.V. (1994) Financial strain and symptoms of depression in a community sample of elderly men and women: a longitudinal study, *Journal of Aging and Health*, 6: 448–68.

Delgado, A.R., Prieto, G. and Bond, R.A. (1997) The cultural factor in lay perception of jealousy as a motive for wife battery, *Journal of Applied Social Psychology*, 27: 1824–41.

Dempsey, K.C. (2000) Men's share of child care: a rural and urban comparison, *Journal of Family Studies*, 6: 245–66.

Denmark, F., Russo, N.F., Frieze, I.H. *et al.* (1988) Guidelines for avoiding sexism in psychological research, *American Psychologist*, 43: 582–5.

DeSouza, E.R., Pierce, T., Zanelli, J.C. and Hutz, C. (1992) Perceived sexual intent in the US and Brazil as a function of nature of encounter, subjects' nationality, and gender, *Journal of Sex Research*, 29: 251–60.

DeSteno, D.A. and Salovey, P. (1996) Evolutionary origins of sex differences in jealousy? Questioning the 'fitness' of the model, *Psychological Science*, 7: 367–72.

Deutsch, F.M. and Saxon, S.E. (1998) Traditional ideologies, nontraditional lives, *Sex Roles*, 38: 331–62.

Deutsch, F.M., Lussier, J.B. and Servis, L.J. (1993) Husbands at home: predictors of paternal participation in childcare and housework, *Journal of Personality and Social Psychology*, 65: 1154–66.

Deutsch, H. (1947) *The Psychology of Women, Volume 2: Motherhood*. London: Love and Malcolmson.

Dixon, P. (1998) Employment factors in conflict in African American heterosexual relationships: some perceptions of women, *Journal of Black Studies*, 28: 491–505.

Dodds, J.P., Nardone, A., Mercey, D. and Johnson, A.M. (2000) Increase in high risk sexual behaviour among homosexual men, London 1996–8: cross sectional, questionnaire study, *British Medical Journal*, 320(7248): 1510–11.

Donovan, B., Minichiello, V. and Hart, G. (1998) STDs in Australia, in T. Brown *et al.*, (eds) *Sexually Transmitted Diseases in Asia and the Pacific*. Honolulu: East–West Centre.

Doress-Worters, P.B. (1994) Adding elder care to women's multiple roles: a critical review of the caregiver stress and multiple roles literatures, *Sex Roles*, 31: 597–616.

Dorfman, R.,Walters, K., Burke, P. *et al.* (1995) Old, sad and alone: the myth of the aging homosexual, *Journal of Gerontological Social Work*, 24: 29–44.

Drewnowski, A., Kurth, C.L. and Krahn, D.D. (1995) Effects of body image on dieting, exercise, and anabolic steroid use in adolescent males, *International Journal of Eating Disorders*, 17: 381–6.

Dubbert, P. and Martin, J. (1988) Exercise, in E.A. Blechman and K.D. Brownell (eds) *Handbook of Behavioral Medicine for Women*. New York: Pergamon.

Dudley, M.J., Kelk, N.J., Florio, T.M. *et al.* (1998) Suicide among young Australians, 1964–1993: an interstate comparison of metropolitan and rural trends, *Medical Journal of Australia*, 169(2): 77–80.

Dunkle, J.H. (1994) Counseling gay male clients: a review of treatment efficacy research: 1975 – present, *Journal of Gay and Lesbian Psychotherapy*, 2: 1–19.

Dutton, D.G., van Ginkel, C. and Landolt, M.A. (1996) Jealousy, intimate abusiveness, and intrusiveness, *Journal of Family Violence*, 11: 411–23.

Duxbury, L. and Higgins, C. (1994) Interference between work and family: a status report on dual-career and dual-earner mothers and fathers, *Employee Assistance Quarterly*, 9: 55–80.

Dworkin, A. (1997) *Life and Death*. New York: Free Press.

Easteal, P. (1993) *Killing the Beloved: Homicide Between Adult Sexual Intimates*, Canberra: Australian Institute of Criminology.

Easteal, P. (1994) Homicide/suicides between adult sexual intimates: an Australian study, *Suicide and Life-Threatening Behavior*, 24: 140–51.

Ehrenberg, M. (1996) Aging and mental health: issues in the gay and lesbian community, in C.J. Alexander *et al.* (eds) *Gay and Lesbian Mental Health: A Sourcebook for Practitioners*. New York: Harrington Park Press.

Emslie, C., Hunt, K. and Macintyre, S. (1999a) Gender differences in minor morbidity among full time employees of a British university, *Journal of Epidemiology and Community Health*, 53: 465–75.

Emslie, C., Hunt, K. and Macintyre, S. (1999b) Problematizing gender, work and health: the relationship between gender, occupational grade, working conditions and minor morbidity in full-time bank employees, *Social Science and Medicine*, 48: 33–48.

Epps, K.J., Haworth, R. and Swaffer, T. (1993) Attitudes toward women and rape among male adolescents convicted of sexual versus nonsexual crimes, *Journal of Psychology*, 127: 501–6.

Erickson, B.M. (1993) *Helping Men Change: The Role of the Female Therapist*. Newbury Park, CA: Sage.

Evans, W.J. (1995) Effects of exercise on body composition and functional capacity of the elderly, *Journals of Gerontology Series A, Biological Sciences and Medical Sciences*, 50A: S147–50.

Fallon, P., Katzman, M.A. and Wooley, S.C. (eds) (1994) *Feminist Perspectives on Eating Disorders*. New York: Guilford Press.

Farrington, D.P. (1998) Predictors, causes, and correlates of male youth violence, *Crime and Justice*, 24: 421–75.

Feeney, A., North, F., Head, J., Canner, R. and Marmot, M. (1998) Socioeconomic and sex differentials in reason for sickness absence from the Whitehall II Study, *Occupational and Environmental Medicine*, 55: 91–8.

Feldman, S., Byles, J.E. and Beaumont, R. (2000) 'Is anybody listening?': the experiences of widowhood for older Australian women, *Journal of Women and Aging*, 12: 155–76.

Feltey, K.M., Ainslie, J.J. and Geib, A. (1991) Sexual coercion attitudes among high school students: the influence of gender and rape education, *Youth and Society*, 23: 229–50.

Felthous, A.R. and Hempel, A. (1995) Combined homicide-suicides: a review, *Journal of Forensic Sciences*, 40: 846–57.

Femiano, S. (1992) The function of affect in therapy with men, *Journal of Men's Studies*, 1: 117–24.

Fennell, G., Phillipson, C. and Evers, H. (1988) *The Sociology of Old Age*. Milton Keynes: Open University Press.

Fergusson, D.M., Horwood, L.J. and Beautrais, A.L. (1999) Is sexual orientation related to mental health problems and suicidality in young people?, *Archives of General Psychiatry*, 56: 876–80.

Ferrara, I., Balet, R. and Grudzinskas, J.G. (2000) Intrauterine donor insemination in single women and lesbian couples: a comparative study of pregnancy rates, *Human Reproduction*, 15: 621–5.

Fichter, M.M., Meller, I., Schroppel, H. and Steinkirchner, R. (1995) Dementia and cognitive impairment in the oldest old in the community: prevalence and comorbidity, *British Journal of Psychiatry*, 166: 621–9.

Field, D. and Minkler, M. (1993) The importance of family in advanced old age: the family is 'forever', in P.A. Cowan *et al.* (eds) *Family, Self, and Society: Toward a New Agenda for Family Research.* Hillsdale, NJ: Lawrence Erlbaum.

Fischer, A. (1993) Sex differences in emotionality: fact or stereotype?, *Feminism and Psychology*, 3: 303–18.

Fisher, M. (1994) Man-made care: community care and older male carers, *British Journal of Social Work*, 24: 659–80.

Fisher, W.A., Boroditsky, R. and Bridges, M.L. (1999) The 1998 Canadian Contraception Study, *Canadian Journal of Human Sexuality*, 8: 161–216.

Fivush, R., Brotman, M.A., Buckner, J.P. and Goodman, S.H. (2000) Gender differences in parent–child emotion narratives, *Sex Roles*, 42: 233–53.

Fletcher, R. (1997) Testosterone poisoning or terminal neglect? The men's health issue. In *Health Issues Papers* 8: 1–33. Canberra: Department of the Parliamentary Librarian.

Florack, E.I., Zielhuis, G.A. and Rolland, R. (1994) Cigarette smoking, alcohol consumption, and caffeine intake and fecundability, *Preventive Medicine*, 23: 175–80.

Flowers, P., Hart, G. and Marriott, C. (1999) Constructing sexual health: gay men and 'risk' in the context of a public sex environment, *Journal of Health Psychology*, 4: 483–95.

Flowers, P., Marriott, C. and Hart, G. (2000) 'The bars, the bogs, and the bushes': the impact of locale on sexual cultures, *Culture, Health and Sexuality*, 2: 69–86.

Ford, J. and Sinclair, R. (1987) *Sixty Years On: Women Talk about Old Age.* London: Women's Press.

Forster, L.E. and Stoller, E.P. (1992) The impact of social support on mortality: a seven-year follow-up of older men and women, *Journal of Applied Gerontology*, 11: 173–86.

Fox, D. and Prilleltensky, I. (eds) (1997) *Critical Psychology: An Introduction.* London: Sage.

Freer, C. (1988) Old myths: frequent misconceptions about the elderly, in N. Wells and C. Freer (eds) *The Ageing Population: Burden or Challenge?* London: Macmillan.

French, S.A., Story, M., Remafedi, G. *et al.* (1996) Sexual orientation and prevalence of body dissatisfaction and eating disordered behaviors: a population-based study of adolescents, *International Journal of Eating Disorders*, 19: 119–26.

Friend, R.A. (1989) Older lesbian and gay people: responding to homophobia, *Marriage and Family Review*, 14: 241–63.

Fuller-Jonap, F. and Haley, W.E. (1995) Mental and physical health of male caregivers of a spouse with Alzheimer's disease, *Journal of Aging and Health*, 7: 99–118.

Furnham, A., Mak, T. and Tanidjojo, L. (2000) An Asian perspective on the portrayal of men and women in television advertisements: studies from Hong Kong and Indonesian television, *Journal of Applied Social Psychology*, 30: 2341–64.

Gabhainn, S.N., Kelleher, C.C., Naughton, A.M. *et al.* (1999) Socio-demographic variations in perspectives on cardiovascular disease and associated risk factors, *Health Education Research*, 14: 619–28.

Galambos, N.L., Petersen, A.C., Richards, M. and Gitelson, I.B. (1985) The Attitudes toward Women Scale for Adolescents (AWSA): a study of reliability and validity. *Sex Roles*, 13: 343–56.

Ganley, A.L. (1988) Feminist therapy with male clients, in M.A. Dutton-Douglas and L.E. Walker (eds) *Feminist Psychotherapies: Integration of Therapeutic and Feminist Systems*. Norwood, NJ: Ablex.

Gardiner, J.P., Judson, J.A., Smith, G.S., Jackson, R. and Norton, R.N. (2000) A decade of intensive care unit trauma admissions in Auckland, *New Zealand Medical Journal*, 113: 327–30.

Gardner, R.M., Friedman, B.N. and Jackson, N.A. (1999) Body size estimations, body dissatisfaction, and ideal size preferences in children six through thirteen, *Journal of Youth and Adolescence*, 28: 603–18.

Garnets, L., Hancock, K.A., Cochran, S.D. *et al.* (1991) Issues in psychotherapy with lesbians and gay men: a survey of psychologists, *American Psychologist*, 46: 964–72.

Garrett-Gooding, J. and Senter, R. (1987) Attitudes and acts of sexual aggression on a university campus, *Sociological Inquiry*, 57: 348–71.

Gatz, M., Harris, J.R. and Turk-Charles, S. (1995) The meaning of health for older women, in A.L. Stanton and S.J. Gallant (eds) *The Psychology of Women's Health: Progress and Challenges in Research and Application*. Washington, DC: American Psychological Association.

Gee, S. and Baillie, J. (1999) Happily ever after? An exploration of retirement expectations, *Educational Gerontology*, 25: 109–28.

Gerberich, S.G., Gibson, R.W., French, L.R. *et al.* (1998) Machinery-related injuries: regional rural injury study-I (RRIS-I), *Accident Analysis and Prevention*, 30: 793–804.

Gijsbers van Wijk, C.M., Huisman, H. and Kolk, A.M. (1999) Gender differences in physical symptoms and illness behavior: a health diary study, *Social Science and Medicine*, 49: 1061–74.

Gilbar, O. and Dagan, A. (1995) Coping with loss: differences between widows and widowers of deceased cancer patients, *Omega Journal of Death and Dying*, 31: 207–20.

Glass, J. (1998) Gender liberation, economic squeeze, or fear of strangers: why fathers provide infant care in dual-earner families, *Journal of Marriage and the Family*, 60: 821–34.

Goldscheier, F.K. (1990) The aging of the gender revolution: what do we know and what do we need to know?, *Research on Aging*, 12: 531–45.

Goldshmidt, O.T. and Weller, L. (2000) 'Talking emotions': gender differences in a variety of conversational contexts, *Symbolic Interaction*, 23: 117–34.

Graham, D.L., Rawlings, E.I., Halpern, H.S. and Hermes, J. (1984) Therapists' needs for training in counseling lesbians and gay men, *Professional Psychology – Research and Practice*, 15: 482–96.

Granello, D.H. (2000) Using a contextual approach in counseling men, *Journal of Psychotherapy in Independent Practice*, 1: 43–52.

Grbich, C.F. (1992) Societal response to familial role change in Australia: marginalisation or social change?, *Journal of Comparative Family Studies*, 23: 79–94.

Grbich, C.F. (1995) Male primary caregivers and domestic labour: involvement or avoidance?, *Journal of Family Studies*, 1: 114–29.

Greenglass, E.R. (1991) Burnout and gender: theoretical and organizational implications, *Canadian Psychology*, 32: 562–74.

Greenglass, E.R., Pantony, K.L. and Burke, R.J. (1988) A gender-role perspective on role conflict, work stress and social support, *Journal of Social Behavior and Personality*, 3: 317–28.

Greif, G.L. (1995) Single fathers with custody following separation and divorce, *Marriage and Family Review*, 20: 213–31.

Grewal, R.P. and Urschel, J.D. (1994) Why women want children: a study during phases of parenthood, *Journal of Social Psychology*, 134: 453–5.

Grice, J.W. and Seely, E. (2000) The evolution of sex differences in jealousy: failure to replicate previous results, *Journal of Research in Personality*, 34: 348–56.

Groth, A.N., Burgess, A.W. and Holstrom, L. (1977) Rape: power, anger and sexuality, *American Journal of Psychiatry*, 134: 1239–43.

Grulich, A. (2000) HIV risk behavior in gay men: on the rise?, *British Medical Journal*, 320(7248): 1487–8.

Gunter, N.C. and Gunter, B.G. (1990) Domestic division of labor among working couples: does androgyny make a difference?, *Psychology of Women Quarterly*, 14: 355–70.

Gupta, S. (1999) The effects of transitions in marital status on men's performance of housework, *Journal of Marriage and the Family*, 61: 700–11.

Hamilton, C. and Denniss, R. (2000) *Tracking Well-being in Australia: The Genuine Progess Indicator 2000*. Canberra: Australia Institute.

Hammig, B.J. and Moranetz, C.A. (2000) Violent victimization: perceptions and preventive behaviors among young adults, *American Journal of Health Behavior*, 24: 143–50.

Hannah, J. and Quarter, J. (1992) Sharing household labour: 'Could you do the bedtime story while I do the dishes?', *Canadian Journal of Community Mental Health*, 11: 147–62.

Hansen, H.L. and Jensen, J. (1998) Female seafarers adopt the high risk lifestyle of male seafarers, *Occupational and Environmental Medicine*, 55: 49–51.

Harding, S. (1986) *The Science Question in Feminism*. Milton Keynes: Open University Press.

Harlow, R.E. and Cantor, N. (1996) Still participating after all these years: a study of life task participation in later life, *Journal of Personality and Social Psychology*, 71: 1235–49.

Harmon, G., Owens, R.G. and Dewey, M.E. (1991) Rapists' and non-rapists' attitudes toward women, *International Journal of Criminology*, 35: 217–24.

Harris, C.E. (2000) Psychophysiological responses to imagined infidelity: the specific innate modular view of jealousy reconsidered, *Journal of Personality and Social Psychology*, 78: 1082–91.

Harris, M.B., Begay, C. and Page, P. (1989) Activities, family relationships and feelings about aging in a multicultural elderly sample, *International Journal of Aging and Human Development*, 29: 103–17.

Harris, M.B., Walters, L.C. and Waschull, S. (1991) Gender and ethnic differences in obesity-related behaviors and attitudes in a college sample, *Journal of Applied Social Psychology*, 21: 1545–66.

Harrison, J., Glass, C.A., Owens, R.G. and Soni, B.M. (1995) Factors associated with sexual functioning in women following spinal cord injury, *Paraplegia*, 33: 687–92.

Hawkins, A.J. and Dollahite, D.C. (eds) (1997) *Generative Fathering: Beyond Deficit Perspectives.* Thousand Oaks, CA: Sage.

Hawkins, A.J. and Eggebeen, D.J. (1991) Are fathers fungible? Patterns of coresident adult men in maritally disrupted families and young children's well-being, *Journal of Marriage and the Family,* 53: 958–72.

Hawkins, A.J., Christiansen, S.L., Sargent, K.P. and Hill, E.J. (1993) Rethinking fathers' involvement in child care: a developmental perspective, *Journal of Family Issues,* 14: 531–49.

Hayward, M.D., Friedman, S. and Chen, H. (1998) Career trajectories and older men's retirement, *Journals of Gerontology Series B, Psychological Sciences and Social Sciences,* 53B: S91–103.

Heeren, T.J., Lagaay, A.M., Hijmans, W. *et al.* (1991) Prevalence of dementia in the 'oldest old' of a Dutch community, *Journal of the American Geriatrics Society,* 39: 755–9.

Heffernan, K. (1994) Sexual orientation as a factor in risk for binge eating and bulimia nervosa: a review, *International Journal of Eating Disorders,* 16: 335–47.

Heffernan, K. (1996) Eating disorders and weight concern among lesbians, *International Journal of Eating Disorders,* 19, 127–38.

Helgeson, V.S. (1995) Masculinity, men's roles, and coronary heart disease, in D.F. Sabo, F. Donald, D.F. Gordon *et al.* (eds) *Men's Health and Illness: Gender, Power, and the Body.* Thousand Oaks, CA: Sage.

Heller, T., Hsieh, K. and Rowitz, L. (1997) Maternal and paternal caregiving of persons with mental retardation across the lifespan, *Family Relations,* 46: 407–15.

Henderson, W.J. and Lyddon, W.J. (1997) Client gender role attitudes and perception of counselor characteristics, *Journal of Mental Health Counseling,* 19: 182–90.

Henriques, G.R. and Calhoun, L.G. (1999) Gender and ethnic differences in the relationship between body esteem and self-esteem, *Journal of Psychology,* 133: 357–68.

Herrell, R., Goldberg, J., True, W.R., Ramakrishnan, V. *et al.* (1999) Sexual orientation and suicidality: a co-twin control study in adult men, *Archives of General Psychiatry,* 56: 867–74.

Hepworth, J. and Griffin, C. (1995) Conflicting opinions? 'Anorexia nervosa', medicine and feminism, in S. Wilkinson and C. Kitzinger (eds) *Feminism and Discourse: Psychological Perspectives.* London: Sage.

Heymann, D. (1995) Sexually transmitted diseases and AIDS: global and regional epidemiology, *Venereology,* 8: 205–10.

Hill, M.S. and Fischer, A.R. (2001) Does entitlement mediate the link between masculinity and rape-related variables?, *Journal of Counseling Psychology,* 48: 39–50.

Hillier, L.M. and Morrongiello, B.A. (1998) Age and gender differences in school-age children's appraisals of injury risk, *Journal of Pediatric Psychology,* 23: 229–38.

Hojat, M. (1990) Can affectional ties be purchased? *Journal of Social Behavior and Personality,* 5: 493–502.

Holcomb, D.R., Holcomb, L.C., Sondag, K.A. and Williams, N. (1991) Attitudes about date rape: gender differences among college students, *College Student Journal,* 25: 434–9.

Holtzman, D., Powell-Griner, E., Bolen, J.C. and Rhodes, L. (2000) State- and sex-specific prevalence of selected characteristics: Behavioral Risk Factor Surveillance System 1996 and 1997, *Morbidity and Mortality Weekly Report: CDC Surveillance Summaries,* 49(6): 1–39.

Holtzworth-Munroe, A., Stuart, G.L. and Hutchinson, G. (1997) Violent versus nonviolent husbands: differences in attachment patterns, dependency, and jealousy, *Journal of Family Psychology*, 11: 314–31.

Hooke, A., Capewell, S. and Whyte, M. (2000) Gender differences in Ayrshire teenagers' attitudes to sexual relationships, responsibility and unintended pregnancies, *Journal of Adolescence*, 23: 477–86.

Hooyman, N.R. and Gonyea, J. (1995) *Feminist Perspectives on Family Care: Policies for Gender Justice*. Thousand Oaks, CA: Sage.

Horne, G., Jamaludin, A., Critchlow, J.D. *et al.* (1998) A 3 year retrospective review of intrauterine insemination, using cryopreserved donor spermatozoa and cycle monitoring by urinary or serum luteinizing hormone measurements, *Human Reproduction*, 13: 3045–8.

Hosea, T.M., Carey, C.C. and Harrer, M.F. (2000) The gender issue: epidemiology of ankle injuries in athletes who participate in basketball, *Clinical Orthopaedics and Related Research*, (372): 45–9.

Hsu, L.K.G. (1990) *Eating Disorders*. New York: Guilford Press.

Hupka, R.B. and Bank, A.L. (1996) Sex differences in jealousy: evolution or social construction?, *Cross-Cultural Research*, 30: 24–59.

International Olympic Committee (IOC) (1999) *Doping: An IOC White Paper*. Lausanne, Switzerland: IOC.

Ishii-Kuntz, M. and Coltrane, S. (1992) Predicting the sharing of household labor: are parenting and housework distinct?, *Sociological Perspectives*, 35: 629–47.

Jacobs, S., Hansen, F., Berkman, L., Kasl, S. and Ostfeld, A. (1989) Depressions of bereavement, *Comprehensive Psychiatry*, 30: 218–24.

Jaeger, M.E. and Rosnow, R.L. (1988) Contextualism and its implications for psychological inquiry, *British Journal of Psychology*, 79: 63–75.

Jahoda, G. (1988) J'accuse, in M.H. Bond (ed.) *The Cross-Cultural Challenge to Social Psychology*. Los Angeles: Sage.

Johnson, J.D., Noel, N.E. and Sutter-Hernandez, J. (2000) Alcohol and male acceptance of sexual aggression: the role of perceptual ambiguity, *Journal of Applied Social Psychology*, 30: 1186–200.

Johnson, M.P. and Puddifoot, J.E. (1996) The grief response in the partners of women who miscarry, *British Journal of Medical Psychology*, 69: 313–27.

Jones, M. (1988) *Secret Flowers: Mourning and the Adaptation to Loss*. London: Women's Press.

Jordan, P.L. (1990) Laboring for relevance: expectant and new fatherhood, *Nursing Research*, 39: 11–16.

Jorm, A.F. (1994) Characteristics of Australians who reported consulting a psychologist for a health problem: an analysis of data from the 1989–90 National Health Survey, *Australian Psychologist*, 29: 212–15.

Jorm, A.F., Korten, A.E. and Henderson, A.S. (1987) The prevalence of dementia: a quantitative integration of the literature, *Acta Psychiatrica Scandinavica*, 76: 465–79.

Jorm, A.F., Christensen, H., Henderson, A.S. *et al.* (1998) Factors associated with successful ageing, *Australian Journal on Ageing*, 17: 33–7.

Kahne, H. (1991) Economic perspectives on work and family issues, in M.T. Notman and C.C. Nadelson (eds) *Women and Men: New Perspectives on Gender Differences*. Washington, DC: American Psychiatric Press.

Kalmijn, M. (1999) Father involvement in childrearing and the perceived stability of marriage, *Journal of Marriage and the Family*, 61: 409–21.

Kandrack, M., Grant, K.R. and Segall, A. (1991) Gender differences in health related behaviour: some unanswered questions, *Social Science and Medicine*, 32: 579–90.

Kanuaha, V.K. (2000) The impact of sexuality and race/ethnicity on HIV/AIDS risk among Asian and Pacific Island American (A/PIA) gay and bisexual men in Hawai'i, *AIDS Education and Prevention*, 12: 505–18.

Karbon, M., Fabes, R.A., Carlo, G. and Martin, C.L. (1992) Preschoolers' beliefs about sex and age differences in emotionality, *Sex Roles*, 27: 377–90.

Katz, D.L., Brunner, R.L., St Jeor, S.T. *et al.* (1998) Dietary fat consumption in a cohort of American adults, 1985–1991: covariates, secular trends, and compliance with guidelines, *American Journal of Health Promotion*, 12: 382–90.

Kawachi, I., Kennedy, B.P. and Wilkinson, R.G. (1999) Crime: social disorganization and relative deprivation, *Social Science and Medicine*, 48: 719–31.

Kaye, L.W. and Applegate, J.S. (1990) *Men as Caregivers to the Elderly: Understanding and Aiding Unrecognised Family Support*. Lexington, MA: Lexington Books.

Kimmel, D.C. (1993) Adult development and aging: a gay perspective, in L.D. Garnets and D.C. Kimmel (eds) *Psychological Perspectives on Lesbian and Gay Male Experiences*. New York: Columbia University Press.

King, V. and Heard, H.E. (1999) Nonresident father visitation, parental conflict, and mother's satisfaction: what's best for child well-being?, *Journal of Marriage and the Family*, 61: 385–96.

Kindlundh, A., Isacson, D., Berglund, L. and Nyberg, F. (1999) Factors associated with adolescent use of doping agents: anabolic-androgenic steroids, *Addiction*, 94: 543–53.

Kinsey, A.C., Pomeroy, W.B. and Martin, C.E. (1948) *Sexual Behavior in the Human Male*. Philadelphia, PA: W.B. Saunders.

Kipnis, D. (1994) Accounting for the use of behavior technologies in social psychology, *American Psychologist*, 49: 165–72.

Kirby, M. (2000) Psychiatry, psychology, law and homosexuality: uncomfortable bedfellows, *Psychiatry, Psychology and Law*, 7: 139–49.

Klonoff, E.A. and Landrine, H. (2000) Is skin color a marker for racial discrimination? Explaining the skin color–hypertension relationship, *Journal of Behavioral Medicine*, 23: 329–38.

Koch, P.B., Boose, L.A., Cohn, M.D. *et al.* (1991) Coping strategies of traditionally and nontraditionally employed women at home and at work, *Health Values: Health Behavior, Education and Promotion*, 15: 19–31.

Kolakowsky-Hayner, S.A., Gourley, E.V., Kreutzer, J.S. *et al.* (1999) Pre-injury substance abuse among persons with brain injury and persons with spinal cord injury, *Brain Injury*, 13: 571–81.

Koss, M.P. (1993) Rape: scope, impact, interventions and public policy responses, *American Psychologist*, 48: 1062–9.

Koss, M.P. and Oros, C.J. (1982) Sexual experiences survey: a research instrument investigating sexual aggression and victimization, *Journal of Consulting and Clinical Psychology*, 50: 455–7.

Kposowa, A.J. (2000) Marital status and suicide in the National Longitudinal Mortality Study, *Journal of Epidemiology and Community Health*, 54: 254–61.

Kring, A.M. and Gordon, A.H. (1998) Sex differences in emotion: expression, experience, and physiology, *Journal of Personality and Social Psychology*, 74: 686–703.

Kroska, A. (1997) The division of labor in the home: a review and conceptualization, *Social Psychology Quarterly*, 60: 304–22.

Krug, E.G., Sharma, G.K. and Lozano, R. (2000) The global burden of injuries, *American Journal of Public Health*, 90: 523–6.

Krull, C. and Trovato, F. (1994) The Quiet Revolution and the sex differential in Quebec's suicide rates: 1931–1986, *Social Forces*, 72: 1121–47.

Kumar, R. (1994) Postnatal mental illness: a transcultural perspective, *Social Psychiatry and Psychiatric Epidemiology*, 29: 250–64.

Kurdek, L.A. (1993) The allocation of household labor in gay, lesbian, and heterosexual married couples, *Journal of Social Issues*, 49: 127–39.

Kvalem, I.L. and Traeen, B. (2000) Self-efficacy, scripts of love and intention to use condoms among Norwegian adolescents, *Journal of Youth and Adolescence*, 29: 337–53.

Lam, L.T., Ross, F.I. and Cass, D.T. (1999) Children at play: the death and injury pattern in New South Wales, Australia, July 1990–June 1994, *Journal of Paediatrics and Child Health*, 35: 572–7.

Lamb, M.E., Pleck, J.H. and Levine, J.A. (1986) Effects of paternal involvement on fathers and mothers, *Marriage and Family Review*, 9(3–4): 67–83.

Landrine, H. (ed.) (1995) *Bringing Cultural Diversity to Feminist Psychology: Theory, Research and Practice*. Washington, DC: American Psychological Association.

Langhinrichsen-Rohling, J., Lewinsohn, P., Rohde, P. *et al.* (1998) Gender differences in the suicide-related behaviors of adolescents and young adults, *Sex Roles*, 39: 839–54.

Larrabee, M.J. (1986) Helping reluctant Black males: an affirmation approach, *Journal of Multicultural Counseling and Development*, 14: 25–38.

Larson, R. and Pleck, J. (1999) Hidden feelings: emotionality in boys and men, *Nebraska Symposium on Motivation*, 45: 25–74.

LeBlanc, A.J., Aneshensel, C.S. and Wight, R.G. (1995) Psychotherapy use and depression among AIDS caregivers, *Journal of Community Psychology*, 23: 127–42.

Lee, C. (1997) Social context, depression and the transition to motherhood, *British Journal of Health Psychology*, 2: 93–108.

Lee, C. (1998a) *Women's Health: Psychological and Social Perspectives*. London: Sage.

Lee, C. (1998b) *Alternatives to Cognition*. Mahwah, NJ: Lawrence Erlbaum.

Lee, C. (1999) Health, stress and coping among women caregivers: a review, *Journal of Health Psychology*, 4: 27–40.

Lee, C. (2001) *Women's Health Australia: What Do We Know? What Do We Need to Know?* Brisbane: Australian Academic Press.

Lee, C.C. (1990) Black male development: counseling the 'Native Son', in D. Moore and F. Leafgren (eds) *Problem Solving Strategies and Interventions for Men in Conflict*. Alexandria, VA: American Association for Counseling and Development.

Lee, C.J., Collins, K.A. and Burgess, S.E. (1999) Suicide under the age of eighteen: a 10-year retrospective study, *American Journal of Forensic Medicine and Pathology*, 20: 27–30.

Lee, G.R., Willetts, M.C. and Seccombe, K. (1998) Widowhood and depression: gender differences, *Research on Aging*, 20: 611–30.

Lee, P.A. (1996) Survey report: concept of penis size, *Journal of Sex and Marital Therapy*, 22: 131–5.

Leidig, M.W. (1992) The continuum of violence against women: psychological and physical consequences, *College Health*, 40: 149–55.

Leonard, R.J. (1996) Complementary activities and multiplex relationships in the life-courses of educated women, *Journal of Family Studies*, 2: 3–14.

Lester, D. (1995) The association between alcohol consumption and suicide and homicide rates: a study of 13 nations, *Alcohol and Alcoholism*, 30: 465–8.

Levant, R.F. (1996) The male code and parenting: a psychoeducational approach, in M.P. Andronico (ed.) *Men in Groups: Insights, Interventions, and Psychoeducational Work*. Washington, DC: American Psychological Association.

Levenson, R.W., Carstensen, L.L. and Gottman, J.M. (1993) Long-term marriage: age, gender, and satisfaction, *Psychology and Aging*, 8: 301–13.

Levy-Skiff, R. (1994) Individual and contextual correlates of marital change across the transition to parenthood, *Developmental Psychology*, 30: 591–601.

Lewis, M. (1985) Older women and health: an overview, *Women and Health*, 10: 1–16.

Li, G. (1995) The interaction effect of bereavement and sex on the risk of suicide in the elderly: an historical cohort study, *Social Science and Medicine*, 40: 825–8.

Li, G. and Baker, S.P. (1996) Exploring the male–female discrepancy in death rates from bicycling injury: the decomposition method, *Accident Analysis and Prevention*, 28: 537–40.

Li, G., Baker, S.P., Langlois, J.A. and Kelen, G.D. (1998) Are female drivers safer? An application of the decomposition method, *Epidemiology*, 9: 379–84.

Li, L. and Ozanne-Smith, J. (2000) Injury hospitalisation rates in Victoria, 1987–97: trends, age and gender patterns, *Australian and New Zealand Journal of Public Health*, 24: 158–65.

Lobo, F. and Watkins, G. (1995) Late career unemployment in the 1990s: its impact on the family, *Journal of Family Studies*, 1: 103–11.

Long, N. (1997) Are we contributing to the devaluation of fathers?, *Clinical Child Psychology and Psychiatry*, 2: 197–9.

Lonnquist, L.E., Weiss, G.L. and Larsen, D.L. (1992) Health value and gender in predicting health protective behavior, *Women and Health*, 19: 69–85.

Lorenz, F.O. (1999) Explaining the higher incidence of adjustment problems among children of divorce compared with those in two-parent families, *Journal of Marriage and the Family*, 61: 1020–33.

Lourens, P.F., Vissers, J.A. and Jessurun, M. (1999) Annual mileage, driving violations, and accident involvement in relation to drivers' sex, age, and level of education, *Accident Analysis and Prevention*, 31: 593–7.

Lovestone, S. and Kumar, R. (1993) Postnatal psychiatric illness: the impact on partners. *British Journal of Psychiatry*, 163: 210–16.

Lubben, J.E. (1988) Gender differences in the relationship of widowhood and psychological well-being among low income elderly, *Women and Health*, 14: 161–89.

Lucas, R.E and Gohm, C.L. (2000) Age and sex differences in subjective well-being across cultures, in E. Diner and E.M. Suh (eds) *Culture and Subjective Well-being*. Cambridge, MA: MIT Press.

Lundberg, U. (1996) Influence of paid and unpaid work on psychophysiological stress responses of men and women, *Journal of Occupational Health Psychology*, 1: 117–30.

Lupton, D. (1998) *The Emotional Self: A Sociocultural Exploration*. London: Sage.

Lupton, D. and Barclay, L. (1997) *Constructing Fatherhood: Discourses and Experiences*. London: Sage.

Lynch, S.M. and Zellner, D.A. (1999) Figure preferences in two generations of men: the use of figure drawings illustrating differences in muscle mass, *Sex Roles*, 40: 833–43.

Lyons, A.C. and Willott, S. (1999) From suet pudding to superhero: representations of men's health for women, *Health*, 3: 283–302.

Mac an Ghaill, M. (ed.) (1996) *Understanding Masculinities: Social Relations and Cultural Arenas*. Buckingham: Open University Press.

McCallum, J., Shadbolt, B. and Wang, D. (1994) Self-rated health and survival: a 7-year follow-up study of Australian elderly, *American Journal of Public Health*, 84: 1100–5.

McConatha, J.T., Lightner, E. and Deaner, S.L. (1994) Culture, age, and gender as variables in the expression of emotions, *Journal of Social Behavior and Personality*, 9: 481–8.

MacDonald, T.K., MacDonald, G., Zanna, M.P. and Fong, G. (2000) Alcohol, sexual arousal, and intentions to use condoms in young men: applying alcohol myopia theory to risky sexual behavior, *Health Psychology*, 19: 290–8.

McDougall, G.J. (1993) Therapeutic issues with gay and lesbian elders, *Clinical Gerontologist*, 14: 45–57.

McGreal, D., Evans, B.J. and Burrows, G.D. (1997) Gender differences in coping following loss of a child through miscarriage or stillbirth: a pilot study, *Stress Medicine*, 13: 159–65.

McHugh, M.C., Koeske, R.D. and Frieze, I.H. (1986) Issues to consider in conducting nonsexist psychological research: a guide for researchers, *American Psychologist*, 41: 879–90.

Macintyre, S. (1993) Gender differences in the perceptions of common cold symptoms, *Social Science and Medicine*, 36: 15–20.

Macintyre, S., Ford, G. and Hunt, K. (1999) Do women 'over-report' morbidity? Men's and women's responses to structured prompting on a standard question on long standing illness, *Social Science and Medicine*, 48: 89–98.

Madden, M.E. (1994) The variety of emotional reactions to miscarriage, *Women and Health*, 21: 85–104.

Major, B. (1993) Gender, entitlement, and the distribution of family labor, *Journal of Social Issues*, 49: 141–59.

Mangweth, B., Pope, H.G., Hudson, J.I. *et al.* (1997) Eating disorders in Austrian men: an intracultural and crosscultural comparison study, *Psychotherapy and Psychosomatics*, 66: 214–21.

Marks, D.F. (1996) Health psychology in context, *Journal of Health Psychology*, 1: 7–21.

Marquart, J.W., Merianos, D.E., Cuvelier, S.J. and Carroll, L. (1996) Thinking about the relationship between health dynamics in the free community and the prison, *Crime and Delinquency*, 42: 331–60.

Marsiglio, W. (ed.) (1995) *Fatherhood: Contemporary Theory, Research, and Social Policy*. Thousand Oaks, CA: Sage.

Marsiglio, W. and Donnelly, D. (1991) Sexual relations in later life: a national study of married persons, *Journals of Gerontology*, 46: S338–44.

Marx, K. (1963) *Selected Writings in Sociology and Social Philosophy* (edited by T.B. Bottomore and M. Rubel). Harmondsworth: Penguin.

Masters, W.H. and Johnson, V. (1970) *Human Sexual Inadequacy*. Boston, MA: Little, Brown.

Mauldin, T. and Meeks, C.B. (1990) Sex differences in children's time use, *Sex Roles*, 22: 537–54.

Messerschmidt, J.W. (1993) *Masculinities and Crime: Critique and Reconceptualization of Theory*. Lanham, MD: Rowman & Littlefield.

Miaskowski, C. (1999) The role of sex and gender in pain perception and responses to treatment, in R.J. Gatchel and D.C. Turk (eds) *Psychosocial Factors in Pain: Critical Perspectives*. New York: Guilford.

Milhausen, R.R. and Herold, E.S. (1999) Does the sexual double standard still exist? Perceptions of university women, *Journal of Sex Research*, 36: 361–8.

Milkie, M.A. and Peltola, P. (1999) Playing all the roles: gender and the work–family balancing act, *Journal of Marriage and the Family*, 61: 476–90.

Milkie, M.A., Simon, R.W. and Powell, B. (1997) Through the eyes of children: youths' perceptions and evaluations of maternal and paternal roles, *Social Psychology Quarterly*, 60: 218–37.

Miller, B. and Marshall, J.C. (1987) Coercive sex on the university campus, *Journal of College Student Personnel*, 28: 38–47.

Millett, K. (1970) *Sexual Politics*. New York: Ballantine.

Mirowsky, J. and Ross, C.E. (1995) Sex differences in distress: real or artifact?, *American Sociological Review*, 60: 449–68.

Moen, P. (1996) A life course perspective on retirement, gender, and well-being, *Journal of Occupational Health Psychology*, 1: 131–44.

Morrison, D.R. (1999) Parental conflict and marital disruption: do children benefit when high-conflict marriages are dissolved? *Journal of Marriage and the Family*, 61: 626–37.

Morrongiello, B.A. and Dawber, T. (2000) Mothers' responses to sons and daughters engaging in injury-risk behaviors on a playground: implications for sex differences in injury rates, *Journal of Experimental Child Psychology*, 76: 89–103.

Morrongiello, B.A. and Rennie, H. (1998) Why do boys engage in more risk taking than girls? The role of attributions, beliefs, and risk appraisals, *Journal of Pediatric Psychology*, 23: 33–43.

Muehlenhard, C.L. and Linton, M.A. (1987) Date rape and sexual aggression in dating situations: incidence and risk factors, *Journal of Consulting Psychology*, 34: 186–96.

Muehlenhard, C.L., Friedman, D.E. and Thomas, C.M. (1985) Is date rape justifiable? The effects of dating activity, who initiated, who paid, and men's attitudes toward women, *Psychology of Women Quarterly*, 9: 297–310.

Mukherjee, S., Carach, C. and Higgins, K. (1997) *A Statistical Profile of Crime in Australia* (Research and Public Policy Series, no. 7). Canberra: Australian Institute of Criminology.

Munnoch, D.A., Darcy, C.M., Whallett, E.J. et al. (2000) Work-related burns in South Wales 1995–96, *Burns*, 26: 565–70.

Murdock, G.P. (1967) *Ethnographic Atlas*. Pittsburgh, PA: University of Pittsburgh Press.

Murgio, A., Fernandez Mila, J., Manolio, A., Maurel, D. and Ubeda, C. (1999) Minor head injury at paediatric age in Argentina, *Journal of Neurosurgical Sciences*, 43: 15–23.

Mutchler, J.E. and Bullers, S. (1994) Gender differences in formal care use in later life, *Research on Aging*, 16: 235–50.

Myers, S.M. and Booth, A. (1996) Men's retirement and marital quality, *Journal of Family Issues*, 17: 336–57.

Nahon, D. and Lander, N.R. (1992) A clinic for men: challenging individual and social myths, *Journal of Mental Health Counseling*, 14: 405–16.

National Campaign Against Violence and Crime (1998) *Fear of Crime, Commonwealth of Australia*. Canberra: Australian Government Publishing Service.

National Health and Medical Research Council of Australia (NHMRC) (1995) *Long-term Effects on Women from Assisted Conception*. Canberra: NHMRC.

National Heart Foundation of Australia (NHFA) (1983) *Risk Factor Prevalence Study No. 2*. Canberra: NHFA.

Newman, P.A. and Zimmerman, M.A. (2000) Gender differences in HIV-related sexual risk behavior among urban African American youth: a multivariate approach, *AIDS Education and Prevention*, 12: 308–25.

Nicolson, P. (1990) A brief report of women's expectations of men's behaviour in the transition to parenthood: contradictions and conflicts for counselling therapy practice, *Counselling Psychology Quarterly*, 3: 353–61.

Nobunaga, A.I., Go, B.K. and Karunas, R.B. (1999) Recent demographic and injury trends in people served by the Model Spinal Cord Injury Care Systems, *Archives of Physical Medicine and Rehabilitation*, 80: 1372–82.

Nowak, J., Mallmin, H. and Larsson, S. (2000) The aetiology and epidemiology of clavicular fractures: a prospective study during a two-year period in Uppsala, Sweden, *Injury*, 31: 353–8.

Office of the Status of Women (1995) *Community Attitudes to Violence Against Women*. Canberra: Office of the Prime Minister and the Cabinet, Australian Government Publishing Service.

Olds, J., Schwartz, R.S., Eisen, S.V. and Betcher, R.W. (1993) Part-time employment and marital well-being: a hypothesis and pilot study, *Family Therapy*, 20: 1–16.

Olivardia, R., Pope, H.G., Mangweth, B. and Hudson, J.I. (1995) Eating disorders in college men, *American Journal of Psychiatry*, 152: 1279–85.

Oliver, M.B. and Hyde, J.S. (1993) Gender differences in sexuality: a meta-analysis, *Psychological Bulletin*, 114: 29–51.

Orbell, S. (1996) Informal care in social context: a social psychological analysis of participation, impact and intervention in care of the elderly, *Psychology and Health*, 11: 155–78.

Ore, T. (1998) Women in the U.S. construction industry: an analysis of fatal occupational injury experience, 1980 to 1992, *American Journal of Industrial Medicine*, 33: 256–62.

Owens, G. (1999) Ethics, aesthetics and empiricism, in P.H. Werhane and A.E. Singer (eds) *Business Ethics in Theory and Practice: Contributions from Asia and New Zealand*. Boston, MA: Kluwer.

Owens, R.G. and Ashcroft, J.B. (1985) *Violence: A Guide for the Caring Professions*. London: Croom Helm.

Paeivaerinta, A., Verkkoniemi, A., Niinistoe, L., Kivelae, S.L. and Sulkava, R. (1999) The prevalence and associates of depressive disorders in the oldest-old Finns, *Social Psychiatry and Psychiatric Epidemiology*, 34: 352–9.

Palsson, B., Stromberg, U., Ohlsson, K. and Skerfving, S. (1998) Absence attributed to incapacity and occupational disease/accidents among female and male workers in the fish-processing industry, *Occupational Medicine*, 48: 289–95.

Papadopoulos, N.G., Stamboulides, P. and Triantafillou, T. (2000) The psychosexual development and behavior of university students: a nationwide survey in Greece, *Journal of Psychology and Human Sexuality*, 11: 93–110.

Parnes, H.S. and Somers, D.G. (1994) Shunning retirement: work experience of men in their seventies and early eighties, *Journal of Gerontology*, 49: S117–24.

Pasley, K. and Minton, C. (1997) Generative fathering after divorce and remarriage: beyond the 'disappearing dad', in A.J. Hawkins and D.C. Dollahite (eds) *Generative Fathering: Beyond Deficit Perspectives*. Thousand Oaks, CA: Sage.

Patterson, T.L., Smith, L.W., Smith, T.L. *et al.* (1992) Symptoms of illness in late adulthood are related to childhood social deprivation and misfortune in men but not in women, *Journal of Behavioral Medicine*, 15: 113–25.

Paul, C., Fitzjohn, J., Herbison, P. and Dickson, N. (2000) The determinants of sexual intercourse before age 16, *Journal of Adolescent Health*, 27: 136–47.

Pennebaker, J.W. (1993) Putting stress into words: health, linguistic, and therapeutic implications, *Behaviour Research and Therapy*, 31: 539–48.

Pennebaker, J.W. (1997) *Opening Up: The Healing Power of Expressing Emotions*. New York: Guilford Press.

Perry-Jenkins, M. (1993) Family roles and responsibilities: what has changed and what has remained the same?, in J. Frankel (ed.) *The Employed Mother and the Family Context*. New York: Springer.

Perry-Jenkins, M. and Crouter, A.C. (1990) Men's provider-role attitudes: implications for household work and marital satisfaction, *Journal of Family Issues*, 11: 136–56.

Peters, A. and Liefbroer, A.C. (1997) Beyond marital status: partner history and well-being in old age, *Journal of Marriage and the Family*, 59: 687–99.

Petersen, A. (1998) *Unmasking the Masculine: 'Men' and 'Identity' in a Sceptical Age*. London: Sage.

Phares, V. (1992) Where's poppa? The relative lack of attention to the role of fathers in child and adolescent psychopathology, *American Psychologist*, 47: 656–64.

Phares, V. (1996) *Fathers and Developmental Psychopathology*. New York: Wiley.

Phares, V. (1999) *'Poppa' Psychology: The Role of Fathers in Children's Mental Wellbeing*. Westport, CT: Praeger/Greenwood.

Philipson, I.J. (1993) *On the Shoulders of Women: The Feminization of Psychotherapy*. New York: Guilford Press.

Pickering, T. (1999) Cardiovascular pathways: socioeconomic status and stress effects on hypertension and cardiovascular function, in N.E. Adler *et al.* (eds) *Socioeconomic Status and Health in Industrial Nations: Social, Psychological, and Biological Pathways*. New York: New York Academy of Sciences.

Piechowski, L.D. (1992) Mental health and women's multiple roles, *Families in Society*, 73: 131–9.

Pines, A.M. and Friedman, A. (1998) Gender differences in romantic jealousy, *Journal of Social Psychology*, 138: 54–71.

Plant, E.A., Hyde, J.S., Keltner, D. and Devine, P.G. (2000) The gender stereotyping of emotions, *Psychology of Women Quarterly*, 24: 81–92.

Pleck, J.H. (1976) The male sex role: definitions, problems, and sources of change, *Journal of Social Issues*, 32: 155–64.

Pleck, J.H. (1977) The work–family role system, *Social Problems*, 24: 417–27.

Pleck, J.H., Lamb, M.E. and Levine, J.A. (1986) Epilog: facilitating future change in men's family roles, *Marriage and Family Review*, 9: 11–16.

Pope, M. and Schulz, R. (1990) Sexual attitudes and behavior in midlife and aging homosexual males, *Journal of Homosexuality*, 20: 169–77.

Popenoe, D. (1993) American family decline 1960–1990: a review and appraisal, *Journal of Marriage and the Family*, 55: 527–42.

Population Reference Bureau (PRB) (2000) *2000 World Population Datasheet*. Washington, DC: PRB, http://www.prb.org/

Porcino, J. (1985) Psychological aspects of aging in women, *Women and Health*, 10: 115–22.

Powell, J.W. and Barber-Foss, K.D. (2000) Sex-related injury patterns among selected high school sports, *American Journal of Sports Medicine*, 28: 385–91.

Pratt, C. and Deosaransingh, K. (1997) Gender differences in homicide in Contra Costa County, California: 1982–1993, *American Journal of Preventive Medicine*, 13(6 suppl.): 19–24.

Price, R.H., Friedland, D.S. and Vinokur, A.D. (1998) Job loss: hard times and eroded identity, in J.H. Harvey (ed.) *Perspectives on Loss: A Sourcebook*. Philadelphia, PA: Brunner/Mazel.

Prilleltensky, I. (1989) Psychology and the status quo, *American Psychologist*, 44: 795–802.

Pritchard, C. (1992) Is there a link between suicide in young men and unemployment? A comparison of the UK with other European Community countries, *British Journal of Psychiatry*, 160: 750–6.

Pruchno, R. and Patrick, J.H. (1999) Mothers and fathers of adults with chronic disabilities, *Research on Aging*, 21: 682–713.

Puddifoot, J.E. and Johnson, M.P. (1997) The legitimacy of grieving: the partner's experience at miscarriage, *Social Science and Medicine*, 45: 837–45.

Puddifoot, J.E. and Johnson, M.P. (1999) Active grief, despair, and difficulty coping: some measured characteristics of male response following their partner's miscarriage, *Journal of Reproductive and Infant Psychology*, 17: 89–93.

Purcell, D.W., Campos, P.E. and Perilla, J.L. (1996) Therapy with lesbians and gay men: a cognitive behavioral perspective, *Cognitive and Behavioral Practice*, 3: 391–415.

Quam, J.K. and Whitford, G.S. (1992) Adaptation and age-related expectations of older gay and lesbian adults, *Gerontologist*, 32: 367–74.

Queensland Domestic Violence Resource Centre (QDVRC) (1992) *Boys Will Be . . . A Report on the Survey of Year Nine Males and their Attitudes to Forced Sex*. Brisbane: QDVRC.

Quick, H.E. and Moen, P. (1998) Gender, employment and retirement quality: a life course approach to the differential experiences of men and women, *Journal of Occupational Health Psychology*, 3: 44–64.

Rapaport, K. and Burkhart, B.R. (1984) Personality and attitudinal characteristics of sexually coercive college males, *Journal of Abnormal Psychology*, 93: 216–21.

Raudenbush, B. and Zellner, D.A. (1997) Nobody's satisfied: effects of abnormal eating behaviors and actual and perceived weight status on body image satisfaction in males and females, *Journal of Social and Clinical Psychology*, 16: 95–110.

Reichle, B. and Gefke, M. (1998) Justice of conjugal divisions of labor: you can't always get what you want, *Social Justice Research*, 11: 271–87.

Reime, B., Novak, P., Born, J., Hagel, E. and Wanek, V. (2000) Eating habits, health status, and concern about health: a study among 1641 employees in the German metal industry, *Preventive Medicine*, 30: 295–301.

Remafedi, G., French, S., Story, M., Resnick, M.D. and Blum, R. (1998) The relationship between suicide risk and sexual orientation: results of a population-based study, *American Journal of Public Health*, 88: 57–60.

Rennemark, M. and Hagberg, B. (1999) Gender specific associations between social network and health behavior in old age, *Aging and Mental Health*, 3: 320–7.

Repetti, R.L., Matthews, K.A. and Waldron, I. (1989) Employment and women's health, *American Psychologist*, 44: 1394–401.

Resnick, M.D., Bearinger, L.H., Stark, P. and Blum, R.W. (1994) Patterns of consultation among adolescent minors obtaining an abortion, *American Journal of Orthopsychiatry*, 64: 310–16.

Rich, A. (1982) *Of Women Born: Motherhood as Experience and Institution*. London: Virago.

Richman, J.A., Raskin, V.D. and Gaines, C. (1991) Gender roles, social support, and postpartum depressive symptomatology: the benefits of caring, *Journal of Nervous and Mental Disease*, 179: 139–47.

Riger, S.C. (1992) Epistemological debates, feminist voices: science, social values and the study of women, *American Psychologist*, 47: 730–40.

Riggs, A. (1997) Men, friends, and widowhood: towards successful aging, *Australian Journal on Ageing*, 16: 182–5.

Rime, B., Philippot P., Boca, S. and Mesquita, B. (1992) Long-lasting cognitive and social consequences of emotion: social sharing and rumination, *European Review of Social Psychology*, 3: 225–58.

Rindfuss, R.R., Cooksey, E.C. and Sutterlin, R.L. (1999) Young adult occupational achievement: early expectations versus behavioral reality, *Work and Occupations*, 26: 220–63.

Risman, B.J. and Johnson-Sumerford, D. (1998) Doing it fairly: a study of postgender marriages, *Journal of Marriage and the Family*, 60: 23–40.

Robinson, M.D. and Johnson, J.T. (1997) Is it emotion or is it stress? Gender stereotypes and the perception of subjective experience, *Sex Roles*, 36: 235–58.

Rodgers, S.J. (1999) Wives' income and marital quality: are there reciprocal effects? *Journal of Marriage and the Family*, 61: 123–32.

Rodin, J. and Ickovics, J.R. (1990) Women's health: review and research agenda as we approach the 21st century, *American Psychologist*, 45: 1018–34.

Rodin, J. and McAvay, G. (1992) Determinants of change in perceived health in a longitudinal study of older adults, *Journal of Gerontology*, 47: P373–84.

Rodin, J., Silberstein, L. and Striegel-Moore, R. (1984) Women and weight: a normative discontent, *Nebraska Symposium on Motivation*, 32: 267–307.

Rosenfield, S. (1989) The effects of women's employment: personal control and sex differences in mental health, *Journal of Health and Social Behavior*, 30: 77–91.

Rosenfield, S. (1992) The costs of sharing: wives' employment and husbands' mental health, *Journal of Health and Social Behavior*, 33: 213–25.

Rothblum, E.D. (1994) 'I'll die for the revolution but don't ask me not to diet': feminism and the continuing stigmatization of obesity, in P. Fallon, M.A. Katzman and S.C. Wooley (eds) *Feminist Perspectives on Eating Disorders*. New York: Guilford.

Rowland, R. (1992) *Living Laboratories: Women and Reproductive Technologies*. Sydney: Pan Macmillan.

Russell, R.J.H. and Wells, P.A. (2000) Predicting marital violence from the Marriage and Relationship Questionnaire: using LISREL to solve an incomplete data problem, *Personality and Individual Differences*, 29: 429–40.

142   The psychology of men's health

Sahl, J.D., Kelsh, M.A., Haines, K.D., Sands, F.K. and Kraus, J. (1997) Acute work injuries among electric utility meter readers, *Epidemiology*, 8: 287–92.

Saintonge, S., Achille, P.A. and Lachance, L. (1998) The influence of Big Brothers on the separation-individuation of adolescents from single-parent families, *Adolescence*, 33: 343–53.

Sanchez, L. (1993) Women's power and the gendered division of domestic labor in the Third World, *Gender and Society*, 63: 434–59.

Savin-Williams, R.C. (1994) Verbal and physical abuse as stressors in the lives of lesbian, gay male, and bisexual youths: associations with school problems, running away, substance abuse, prostitution, and suicide, *Journal of Consulting and Clinical Psychology*, 62: 261–9.

Savin-Williams, R.C. and Diamond, L.M. (2000) Sexual identity trajectories among sexual-minority youths: gender comparisons, *Archives of Sexual Behavior*, 29: 607–27.

Schappert, S.M. (1999) Ambulatory care visits to physician offices, hospital outpatient departments, and emergency departments: United States 1997, *Vital and Health Statistics – Series 13: Data from the National Health Survey*, November: 1–39.

Schiavi, R.C. (1990) Sexuality and aging in men, *Annual Review of Sex Research*, 1: 227–49.

Schmidt, G., Klusmann, D., Dekker, A. and Matthiesen, S. (1998) Changes in students' sexual behaviour: 1966–1981–1996: a first report on a longitudinal study in West Germany, *Scandinavian Journal of Sexology*, 1: 157–73.

Schneider, D.S., Sledge, P.A., Shuchter, S.R. and Zisook, S. (1996) Dating and remarriage over the first two years of widowhood, *Annals of Clinical Psychiatry*, 8: 51–7.

Schneider, J.A., O'Leary, A. and Jenkins, S.R. (1995) Gender, sexual orientation, and disordered eating, *Psychology and Health*, 10: 113–28.

Schofield, M.J., Mishra, G. and Dobson, A. (2000) Risk of multiple miscarriages among middle aged women who smoke, in R. Lu et al. (eds), *Tobacco: The Growing Epidemic*. London: Springer.

Schut, H.A.W., Stroebe, M.S. and van den Bout, J. (1997) Intervention for the bereaved: gender differences in the efficacy of two counselling programmes, *British Journal of Clinical Psychology*, 36: 63–72.

Schwerin, M.J., Corcoran, K.J., LaFleur, B.J. et al. (1996) Psychological predictors of anabolic steroid use: an exploratory study, *Journal of Child and Adolescent Substance Abuse*, 6: 57–68.

Seeman, T.E. (1994) Successful aging: reconceptualizing the aging process from a more positive perspective, in B. Vellas and J.L. Albarade (eds) *Facts and Research in Gerontology 1994: Epidemiology and Aging*. New York: Springer.

Segal, L. (1990) *Slow Motion: Changing Masculinities, Changing Men*. London: Virago.

Shannon, J.W. and Woods, W.J. (1991) Affirmative psychotherapy for gay men, *Counseling Psychologist*, 19: 197–215.

Shapiro, A. and Lambert, J.D. (1999) Longitudinal effects of divorce on the quality of the father–child relationship and on fathers' psychological well-being, *Journal of Marriage and the Family*, 61: 397–408.

Sharp, M. and Collins, D. (1998) Exploring the 'inevitability' of the relationship between anabolic-androgenic steroid use and aggression in human males, *Journal of Sport and Exercise Psychology*, 20: 379–94.

Sharpe, P.A. (1995) Older women and health services: moving from ageism toward empowerment, *Women and Health*, 22: 9–23.

Shotland, R.L. and Goodstein, L. (1983) Just because she doesn't want to doesn't mean it's rape: an experimentally based causal model of the perception of rape in a dating situation, *Social Psychology Quarterly*, 46: 220–32.

Shye, D., Mullooly, J.P., Freeborn, D.K. and Pope, C.R. (1995) Gender differences in the relationship between social network support and mortality: a longitudinal study of an elderly cohort, *Social Science and Medicine*, 41: 935–47.

Siever, M.D. (1994) Sexual orientation and gender as factors in socioculturally acquired vulnerability to body dissatisfaction and eating disorders, *Journal of Consulting and Clinical Psychology*, 62: 252–60.

Silverberg, R.A. (1984) Reality Therapy with men: an action approach, *Journal of Reality Therapy*, 3: 27–31.

Skinner, B.F. (1975) The steep and thorny way to a science of behavior, *American Psychologist*, 30: 42–9.

Skinner, W.F. (1994) The prevalence and demographic predictors of illicit and licit drug use among lesbians and gay men, *American Journal of Public Health*, 84: 1307–10.

Slade, P.D. (1982) Towards a functional analysis of anorexia nervosa and bulimia nervosa, *British Journal of Clinical Psychology*, 21: 167–79.

Slater, R. (1995) *The Psychology of Growing Old: Looking Forward*. Buckingham: Open University Press.

Slive, Z.S. (1986) The feminist therapist and the male client, *Women and Therapy*, 5: 81–7.

Smith, C.D. (1998) 'Men don't do this sort of thing': a case study of the social isolation of househusbands, *Men and Masculinities*, 1: 138–72.

Smith, D.E., Thompson, J.K., Raczynski, J.M. and Hilner, J.E. (1999) Body image among men and women in a biracial cohort: the CARDIA study, *International Journal of Eating Disorders*, 25: 71–82.

Smith, D.W.E. (1993) *Human Longevity*. Oxford: Oxford University Press.

Smith, J. and Baltes, M.M. (1998) The role of gender in very old age: profiles of functioning and everyday life patterns, *Psychology and Aging*, 13: 676–95.

Smith, K.R. and Zick, C.D. (1996) Risk of mortality following widowhood: age and sex differences by mode of death, *Social Biology*, 43: 59–71.

Smith, P. and Welchans, S. (2000) Peer education: does focusing on male responsibility change sexual assault attitudes?, *Violence Against Women*, 6: 1255–68.

Smyth, J.M. (1998) Written emotional expression: effect sizes, outcome types, and moderating variables, *Journal of Consulting and Clinical Psychology*, 66: 174–84.

Snedecor, M.R., Boudreau, C.F., Ellis, B.E. *et al.* (2000) U.S. Air force recruit injury and health study, *American Journal of Preventive Medicine*, 18(3 suppl.): 129–40.

Social Trends (1995) *Social Trends on CD-ROM: Version 1.0*. London: Central Statistical Office.

Sorenson, S.B. and White, J.W. (1992) A sociocultural view of sexual assault: from discrepancy to diversity, *Journal of Social Issues*, 48: 187–95.

South, S.J. and Spitze, G. (1994) Housework in marital and nonmarital households, *American Sociological Review*, 59: 327–47.

Spence, J.T. (1985) Achievement American style, *American Psychologist*, 40: 1275–95.

Stanton, A.L. (1995) Psychology of women's health: barriers and pathways to knowledge, in A.L. Stanton and S.J. Gallant (eds) *The Psychology of Women's*

Health: Progress and Challenges in Research and Application. Washington, DC: American Psychological Association.

Stanton, A.L. and Gallant, S.J. (1995) Psychology of women's health: challenges for the future, in A.L. Stanton and S.J. Gallant (eds) *The Psychology of Women's Health: Progress and Challenges in Research and Application.* Washington, DC: American Psychological Association.

Stevens, G. and Gardner, S. (1994) *Separation Anxiety and the Dread of Abandonment in Adult Males.* Westport, CT: Praeger/Greenwood.

Stevens, J.A., Hasbrouck, L.M., Durant, T.M. *et al.* (1999) Surveillance for injuries and violence among older adults, *Morbidity and Mortality Weekly Report: CDC Surveillance Summaries*, 48(8): 27–50.

Stevenson, H., Webster, J., Johnson, R. and Beynnon, B. (1998) Gender differences in knee injury epidemiology among competitive alpine ski racers, *Iowa Orthopaedic Journal*, 18: 64–6.

Stoller, E.P. and Cutler, S.J. (1992) The impact of gender on configurations of care among married elderly couples, *Research on Aging*, 14: 313–30.

Stone, K.E., Lanphear, B.P., Pomerantz, W.J. and Khoury, J. (2000) Childhood injuries and deaths due to falls from windows, *Journal of Urban Health*, 77: 26–33.

Story, M., French, S.A., Resnick, M.D. and Blum, R.W. (1995) Ethnic/racial and socioeconomic differences in dieting behaviours and body image perceptions in adolescents, *International Journal of Eating Disorders*, 18: 173–9.

Stoverinck, M.J., Lagro-Janssen, A.L. and Weel, C.V. (1996) Sex differences in health problems, diagnostic testing, and referral in primary care, *Journal of Family Practice*, 43: 567–76.

Strawbridge, W.J., Camacho, T.C., Cohen, R.D. and Kaplan, G.A. (1993) Gender differences in factors associated with change in physical functioning in old age: a 6-year longitudinal study, *Gerontologist*, 33: 603–9.

Striegel-Moore, R. (1994) A feminist agenda for psychological research on eating disorders, in P. Fallon, M.A. Katzman and S.C. Wooley (eds) *Feminist Perspectives on Eating Disorders.* New York: Guilford.

Stroebe, M.S. (1998) New directions in bereavement research: exploration of gender differences, *Palliative Medicine*, 12: 5–12.

Stronegger, W.J., Freidl, W. and Rasky, E. (1997) Health behaviour and risk behaviour: socioeconomic differences in an Austrian rural county, *Social Science and Medicine*, 44: 423–6.

Szinovacz, M. and Washo, C. (1992) Gender differences in exposure to life events and adaptation to retirement, *Journal of Gerontology*, 47: S191–6.

Taylor, R., Morrell, S., Slaytor, E. and Ford, P. (1998) Suicide in urban New South Wales, Australia 1985–1994: socio-economic and migrant interactions, *Social Science and Medicine*, 47: 1677–86.

Thomas, J.L. (1994) Older men as fathers and grandfathers, in E.H. Thompson (ed.) *Older Men's Lives.* Thousand Oaks, CA: Sage.

Thompson, E.H. (1996) *Men and Aging: A Selected, Annotated Bibliography.* Westport, CT: Greenwood Press.

Thompson, L. (1991) Family work: women's sense of fairness, *Journal of Family Issues*, 12: 181–96.

Thompson, L.W., Gallagher-Thompson, D., Futterman, A., Gilewski, M.J. and Peterson, J. (1991) The effects of late-life spousal bereavement over a 30-month interval, *Psychology and Aging*, 6: 434–41.

Thompson, M.J. (2000) Gender in magazine advertising: skin sells best, *Clothing and Textiles Research Journal*, 18: 178–81.

Thompson, R.A. and Amato, P.R. (eds) (1999) *The Postdivorce Family: Children, Parenting, and Society*. Thousand Oaks, CA: Sage.

Thompson, S.H., Corwin, S.J. and Sargent, R.G. (1997) Ideal body size beliefs and weight concerns of fourth-grade children, *International Journal of Eating Disorders*, 21: 279–84.

Thorn, G.R. and Sarata, B.P.V. (1998) Psychotherapy with African American men: what we know and what we need to know, *Journal of Multicultural Counseling and Development*, 26: 240–53.

Thuen, F. (1997) Received social support from informal networks and professionals in bereavement, *Psychology, Health and Medicine*, 2: 51–63.

Tiggemann, M. and Wilson-Barrett, E. (1998) Children's figure ratings: relationship to self-esteem and negative stereotyping, *International Journal of Eating Disorders*, 23: 83–8.

Timmers, M., Fischer, A.H. and Manstead, A.S.R. (1998) Gender differences in motives for regulating emotions, *Personality and Social Psychology Bulletin*, 24: 974–85.

Traustadottir, R. (1991) Mothers who care: gender, disability and family life, *Journal of Family Issues*, 12: 211–18.

Treas, J. and Giesen, D. (2000) Sexual infidelity among married and cohabiting Americans, *Journal of Marriage and the Family*, 62: 48–60.

Troth, A. and Peterson, C.C. (2000) Factors predicting safe-sex talk and condom use in early sexual relationships, *Health Communication*, 12: 195–218.

Uitenbroek, D.G., Kerekovska, A. and Festchieva, N. (1996) Health lifestyle behaviour and socio-demographic characteristics: a study of Varna, Glasgow and Edinburgh, *Social Science and Medicine*, 43: 367–77.

Umberson, D. (1992) Gender, marital status and the social control of health behavior, *Social Science and Medicine*, 34: 907–17.

Umberson, D., Wortman, C.B. and Kessler, R.C. (1992) Widowhood and depression: explaining long-term gender differences in vulnerability, *Journal of Health and Social Behavior*, 33: 10–24.

US Bureau of Labor Statistics (1991) *Employment and Earnings, January 1991*, 38(1). Washington, DC: US Government Printing Office.

US Bureau of the Census (1993) Primary child care arrangements used by employed mothers for children under 5 years 1977 to 1991, *Current Population Reports, Series P-23*, no. 610. Washington, DC: US Government Printing Office.

Ussher, J.M. (1990) Couples therapy with gay clients: issues facing counsellors, *Counselling Psychology Quarterly*, 3: 109–16.

Ussher, J.M. (1997) *Fantasies of Femininity: Reframing the Boundaries of Sex*. New Brunswick, NJ: Rutgers University Press.

Valentine, D.P. (1986) Psychological impact of infertility: identifying issues and needs, *Social Work in Health Care*, 11(4): 61–9.

van Asbeck, F.W., Post, M.W. and Pangalila, R.F. (2000) An epidemiological description of spinal cord injuries in The Netherlands in 1994, *Spinal Cord*, 38: 420–4.

van Grootheest, D.S., Beekman, A.T.F., van Groenou, M.I. et al. (1999) Sex differences in depression after widowhood: do men suffer more?, *Social Psychiatry and Psychiatric Epidemiology*, 34: 391–8.

Victoria Police (1997) *Crime Statistics 1995/96*, Melbourne: Victoria Police Family Violence Project Office.

Voydanoff, P. and Donnelly, B.W. (1999) The intersection of time in activities and perceived unfairness in relation to psychological distress and marital quality, *Journal of Marriage and the Family*, 61: 739–51.

Waldron, I. (1997) Changing gender roles and gender differences in health behavior, in D.S. Gochman (ed.) *Handbook of Health Behavior Research, Vol. 1: Personal and Social Determinants*. New York: Plenum.

Wallace, J.E. (1996) Gender differences in beliefs of why women live longer than men, *Psychological Reports*, 79: 587–91.

Walzer, S. (1996) Thinking about the baby: gender and divisions of infant care, *Social Problems*, 43: 219–34.

Watson, J. (2000) *Male Bodies: Health, Culture and Identity*. Buckingham: Open University Press.

Watson, W.L. and Ozanne-Smith, J. (2000) Injury surveillance in Victoria, Australia: developing comprehensive injury incidence estimates, *Accident Analysis and Prevention*, 32: 277–86.

Wearing, B. (1984) *The Ideology of Motherhood*. Sydney: Allen & Unwin.

Webb, R.E. and Daniluk, J.C. (1999) The end of the line: infertile men's experiences of being unable to produce a child, *Men and Masculinities*, 2: 6–25.

Weisbuch, J.B. (1991) The new responsibility for prison health: working with the public health community, *Journal of Prison and Jail Health*, 10: 3–18.

Welander, G., Ekman, R., Svanstrom, L., Schelp, L. and Karlsson, A. (1999) Bicycle injuries in Western Sweden: a comparison between counties, *Accident Analysis and Prevention*, 31(1–2): 13–19.

Wells, N. and Freer, C. (1988) Introduction, in N. Wells and C. Freer (eds) *The Ageing Population: Burden or Challenge?* London: Macmillan.

Wells, Y. and Stacey, B. (1998) Gender differences in depressive symptoms among older people living in the community, *Australian Journal on Ageing*, 17: 193–201.

Welsh, M.C., Robinson, T.L. and Lindman, L.S. (1998) Sex differences in health attitudes and choice of health behaviors, *Psychological Reports*, 83: 1161–2.

Werner-Wilson, R.J., Price, S.J., Zimmerman, T.S. and Murphy, M.J. (1997) Client gender as a process variable in marriage and family therapy: are women clients interrupted more than men clients?, *Journal of Family Psychology*, 11: 373–7.

West, A. (1998) The piloting of a group for the fathers of children with Down syndrome, *Child: Care, Health and Development*, 24: 289–94.

Wetle, T. (1991) Successful aging: new hope for optimizing mental and physical well-being, *Journal of Geriatric Psychiatry*, 24: 3–12.

White, N.R. (1994) About fathers: masculinity and the social construction of fatherhood, *Australian and New Zealand Journal of Sociology*, 30: 119–31.

Wilcox, S. (1997) Age and gender in relation to body attitudes: is there a double standard of aging?, *Psychology of Women Quarterly*, 21: 549–65.

Wilkie, J.R., Ferree, M.M. and Ratcliff, K.S. (1998) Gender and fairness: marital satisfaction in two-earner couples, *Journal of Marriage and the Family*, 60: 577–94.

Wilkinson, S. (1996) Feminist social psychologies: a decade of development, in S. Wilkinson (ed.) *Feminist Social Psychologies: International Perspectives*. Buckingham: Open University Press.

Willén, H. (1994) How do couples decide about having their first child? An explorative study, *Göteborg Psychological Reports*, 24(1): 1–40.

Williams, J.M., Wright, P., Currie, C.E. and Beattie, T.F. (1998) Sports related injuries in Scottish adolescents aged 11–15, *British Journal of Sports Medicine*, 32: 291–6.

Williams, M.L., Elwood, W.N. and Bowen, A.M. (2000) Escape from risk: a qualitative exploration of relapse to unprotected anal sex among men who have sex with men, *Journal of Psychology and Human Sexuality*, 11: 25–49.

Willott, S. and Griffin, C. (1997) 'Wham bam, am I a man?': unemployed men talk about masculinities, *Feminism and Psychology*, 7: 107–28.

Wisocki, P.A. and Skowron, J. (2000) The effects of gender and culture on adjustment to widowhood, in R.M. Eisler and M. Hersen (eds) *Handbook of Gender, Culture, and Health*. Mahwah, NJ: Lawrence Erlbaum.

Wladis, A., Bostrom, L. and Nilsson, B. (1999) Unarmed violence-related injuries requiring hospitalization in Sweden from 1987 to 1994, *Journal of Trauma-Injury Infection and Critical Care*, 47: 733–7.

Wolinsky, F.D. and Johnson, R.J. (1992) Perceived health status and mortality among older men and women, *Journals of Gerontology*, 47: S304–12.

Wong, T.Y., Lincoln, A., Tielsch, J.M. and Baker, S.P. (1998) The epidemiology of ocular injury in a major US automobile corporation, *Eye*, 12: 870–4.

Woods, E.R., Lin, Y.G., Middleman, A. *et al.* (1997) The associations of suicide attempts in adolescents, *Pediatrics*, 99: 791–6.

Wooley, O.W. (1994) . . . And man created 'woman': representations of women's bodies in Western culture, in P. Fallon, M.A. Katzman and S.C. Wooley (eds) *Feminist Perspectives on Eating Disorders*. New York: Guilford.

Wright, E.O., Shire, K., Hwang, S. *et al.* (1992) The non-effects of class on the gender division of labor in the home: a comparative study of Sweden and the United States, *Gender and Society*, 62: 252–82.

Wroblewska, A.M. (1997) Androgenic-anabolic steroids and body dysmorphia in young men, *Journal of Psychosomatic Research*, 42: 225–34.

Wu, Z. (1995) Remarriage after widowhood: a marital history study of older Canadians, *Canadian Journal on Aging*, 14: 719–36.

Wyke, S., Hunt, K. and Ford, G. (1998) Gender differences in consulting a general practitioner for common symptoms of minor illness, *Social Science and Medicine*, 46: 901–6.

Yip, P.S. (1998) Suicides in Hong Kong and Australia, *Crisis*, 19: 24–34.

Yip, P.S., Chi, I. and Yu, K.K. (1998) An epidemiological profile of elderly suicides in Hong Kong, *International Journal of Geriatric Psychiatry*, 13: 631–7.

Yip, P.S., Callanan, C. and Yuen, H.P. (2000) Urban/rural and gender differentials in suicide rates: east and west, *Journal of Affective Disorders*, 57: 99–106.

Zelkowitz, P. and Milet, T.H. (1997) Stress and support as related to postpartum paternal mental health and perceptions of the infant, *Infant Mental Health Journal*, 18: 424–35.

Zimbardo, P.G. and Leippe, M.R. (1991) *The Psychology of Attitude Change and Social Influence*. New York: McGraw-Hill.

Zipp, A. and Holcomb, C.A. (1992) Living arrangements and nutrient intakes of healthy women aged 65 and older: a study in Manhattan, Kansas, *Journal of Nutrition for the Elderly*, 11: 1–18.

Zisook, S. and Shuchter, S.R. (1991) Early psychological reaction to the stress of widowhood, *Psychiatry*, 54: 320–33.

Index